Henry Blake Fuller

The puppet-booth

twelve plays

Henry Blake Fuller

The puppet-booth
twelve plays

ISBN/EAN: 9783743322134

Manufactured in Europe, USA, Canada, Australia, Japa

Cover: Foto ©Thomas Meinert / pixelio.de

Manufactured and distributed by brebook publishing software
(www.brebook.com)

Henry Blake Fuller

The puppet-booth

THE PUPPET-BOOTH

TWELVE PLAYS

BY

HENRY B. FULLER

AUTHOR OF "THE CHATELAINE OF LA TRINITÉ,"
"THE CHEVALIER OF PENSIERI-VANI," ETC.

NEW YORK
THE CENTURY CO.
1896

CONTENTS

THE CURE OF SOULS.

PERSONS.

The Sinner.

The Saint.

The Hermit.

The Ignoramus.

The Woman Worldly Wise.

A Series of Dumb Shows.

Ballet Infernal.

A pool in the heart of the primeval forest. Close beside
it, a human habitation — half lodge, half chapel. The
pool is fed by a small stream which, rising high above,
forms a waterfall over a ledge of rock; and it is emptied
by means of a wider stream which flows into a lake lying
many feet below. Close to the edge of the pool a flock
of lambs are grazing, and two or three swans, with their
young, float upon its surface. The spot is closed in by a
chain of mountain-peaks pink in the latest moment of the
sunset glow, and upon the lightly ruffled bosom of the
pool itself one sees the dancing double of the evening star.

Present: the Saint and the Sinner. She is robed in
a fluttering tissue of celestial blue; he is clad in peniten-
tial garb and reclines on a rustic couch beside which rests
his harp; he has left some of his best years behind him,
and his face shows the scars and flushes of a hundred
strange sins.

1

The SAINT. If I may not dress your wound, I may at least sing to you?

The SINNER. Ay, sing,— as I would sing to you, were not my arm all powerless and my poor harp all tuneless and unstrung. Sing; that will dress my spiritual wounds;— for the one wound in view, I have a score within.

The SAINT. Let us hope that your harp will one day attune itself anew.— What shall my song be? Shall I sing to the evening star or to my spinning-wheel?

The SINNER. You have a spinning-wheel?

The SAINT. Yes; else these lambs and their fleece would go for naught.

The SINNER. Are the lambs yours?

The SAINT. I call them mine; but in truth they belong to a wise woman who dwells farther within the recesses of the forest.

The SINNER. Why apart from you?

The SAINT. To escape the sound of my bell.

The SINNER. She objects to it?

The SAINT. She allows it to me.

The SINNER. Is she a friend?

The SAINT. I have not yet found her an enemy.

The SINNER. You spin for her, then — and willingly?

The SAINT. I might do worse.

The SINNER. You do not love her. Why do you remain here?

The SAINT. She speaks of a world outside — a world all wide and wicked.

The SINNER. How much has she told you about it?

The SAINT. Very little. She threatens me with knowledge of it on days when I seem careless or idle.

The SINNER. You do not wish to learn what she can tell you?

The SAINT. Not for worlds — not for all the worlds there are!

The SINNER (*with a start of joy*). Ah, then I have found you at last; my search and my sufferings end here.— Come, sing; sing to your wheel. The stars can sing together, of themselves; — together, and possibly apart. The poor un-aided wheel is dumb.

[The SAINT seats herself at her wheel and softly croons a little melody.]

The SINNER. Ah, to listen to that was well worth the climb. How many *do* climb to this place?

The SAINT. Very few.

The SINNER. Am I the first?

The SAINT. Almost. Many, I am told, are they who dwell at the foot of the mountain and drink of the waters of the salt sea . . .

The SINNER. I was one of them for years. I did not like the draught, but I was loath to strive for betterment.

The SAINT. And there are those, too, who come up as far as the lake beneath us. Few rise higher. A hermit dwells there who tells them that they are satisfied.

The SINNER. I have drunk of his waters and have tried to believe in his words. But neither met my needs.

The SAINT. A few leave him below and clamber up to this pool. Here is *my* ministry.

The SINNER. Your pool is better than his lake, but there must be something better still.

The SAINT. There is: the spring above us, which makes the fall and feeds the pool and helps to form the great sea itself. To this spring I lead such as may desire.

The SINNER. You shall lead me to it, when I am stronger — unless I am too wicked to approach it.

The SAINT. How wicked are you?

The SINNER. I am the sum of all wickednesses.

The SAINT. Tell me some of them.

The SINNER. But you have refused to hear them.

The SAINT. From my wise woman — yes. But it would be different coming from you.

The SINNER. If I were to tell you truly, your chaste eyes —

The SAINT. Must my chaste eyes be forever content with the snow-peaks reflected in my pool? Your eyes — how different they are! — they glitter and burn; they scintillate with the unseen sights of the universe.

The SINNER. And your pure cheeks —

The SAINT. I have already seen them flush a hundred times in my faithful mirror spread out here before us. But it is your cheeks that I regard. They are yet young, but they are seared and scarred, and one may well wonder what has made them so.

The SINNER. But do not ask. Else your timid ears —

The SAINT. My ears — I have almost forgotten their uses. They hear little save the rustling of the trees, the lapping of these waters, the bleating of yonder lambs. But yours — yours have heard a thousand things that stab and sting . . .

The SINNER. You are right. For I have lived, and I have helped a few others to live too. And many more to die.

The SAINT. To die?

The SINNER. Yes; for the wrongs I have wrought have not been wrought upon myself alone. If you could but know of the evil that follows upon the exercise of unre-

stricted power, upon the unhampered wreaking of one's
own will . . .

The SAINT. Tell me.

The SINNER. No, no; I dare not. I must be silent —
alike for your sake and for my own.

[Nevertheless, the misty veil of the waterfall is parted
and reveals a rocky recess behind it. The walls of this
recess take upon themselves the semblance of a subter-
ranean dungeon; a rack is visible, and close beside it a
figure like that of the SINNER himself directs the horrible
procedure of the torture-chamber. At the same time a
wild cry is heard.]

The SINNER (*starting*). What is that sound? (*He turns
suddenly and sees the spectacle behind the waterfall. Then,
to the* SAINT:) No, no; you need not look that way. The
cry was not behind us; it was overhead. (*The waterfall,
resuming its earlier course, shuts out the view of the cavern.*)
Look up, look up! — an eagle slowly circling in the sky
above us.

The SAINT. I see him. I pray he may do no harm.

The SINNER. He is selfish — like every other creature;
he will snatch what he requires. If you could but know
the deadly length to which the self-seeker may go . . .

The SAINT. Tell me.

The SINNER. No, no; I dare not. I must be silent —
alike for your sake and for my own.

[Notwithstanding this, the veil of the waterfall parts a
second time and reveals a shipwreck festering on a wide
waste of stagnant waters. Two living figures struggle
feebly for the last crumb of bread and the last drop of

water. One of them, in the likeness of the SINNER himself, stabs the other and pushes his body overboard into
the sea.]

The SINNER (*groaning deeply, after having cast a sidelong
glance in the direction of the waterfall*). Oh! oh! Might
I but forget it!

The SAINT. You are in pain. Your wound again begins to burn?

The SINNER. And to bleed. But it is a wound whose
gash you cannot see, whose fever you cannot feel. For I
have done — *that;* ay, worse — far worse — than that.
If you could but know the heights to which an insensate
fury can rise . . .

The SAINT. Tell me.

The SINNER. No, no; I dare not. I must be silent —
alike for your sake and for my own.

[But his silence does not prevent the parting of the
watery veil for yet a third time. There appears the street
of a city given over to sack and slaughter. A frenzied
figure, like that of the SINNER's self, rushes hither and
thither with a dripping sword, and the pavement is red
with the blood of defenseless women and of suckling in-
fants. Again a cry is heard — louder and more piercing.]

The SINNER (*placing himself between the* SAINT *and the
waterfall*). No! Look, rather, there. (*He points to the
farther side of the pool.*)

The SAINT. He is swooping down! My poor swans
— can nothing save them? Come, let us hasten round . . .

The SINNER. Ay, let us rescue one innocent, at least.
Let me atone now for the ruthless sacrifices of other days.

[He rises with a sudden start. But his wound breaks out afresh and his bandages are dyed with blood. He sinks back panting.]

The SINNER. Too late! too late! I cannot serve you.

The SAINT. Too late! too late! We cannot save it. See yon poor cygnet borne away, leaving nothing behind but a few fluttering feathers and a few pitiful drops of blood!

The SINNER. I am too evil to be permitted one work of good. I am worse, far worse, than you can know. If you could but conceive the depths into which a man may be plunged by uncontrollable passion. . . .

The SAINT. Tell me. I could forgive you.

The SINNER. No, no; I must be silent. For you shall do much more than merely to forgive.

[Yet the merciless veil of the waterfall parts for a fourth time. It reveals an orgy in a vast and splendid banquet hall. A figure like that of the SINNER forms the center of the revel; one arm holds aloft a wine-cup; the other encircles a jeweled wanton's waist.]

A VOICE. Tell her; tell her.

[The WOMAN WORLDLY WISE advances from the edge of the darkening forest.]

The SINNER (*groaning in anguish alike of body and of spirit*). No, no!

The WOMAN WORLDLY WISE. I understand who and what you are. I have heard of your pilgrimage through our forest. You did well to pass that hermit by. For you seek redemption — is it not true?

The SINNER. Yes.

The WOMAN WORLDLY WISE. Then let all be confessed; let all be known. For knowledge is the way to redemption.

The SINNER. You are wrong. I know too much already. Knowledge is the way to damnation.

The WOMAN WORLDLY WISE. Will ignorance heal your wound? Never. Acknowledge all, and I will cure you. Tell me everything, or I will tell — her. And then her ignorance — at last enlightened — will be powerless to help you.

The SINNER. Ah, you have confirmed my highest hopes! Know, in return, that I depend not upon ignorance, but upon innocence.

The WOMAN WORLDLY WISE. They are the same.— Look, girl! (*She points to the waterfall, where the orgy still proceeds at an ever-mounting, ever-maddening pace.*)

The SINNER. No, no; do not look, I beg you! If you do, it will be your ruin, and mine as well!

[The SAINT, despite herself, turns her eyes toward the waterfall, which she contemplates long and earnestly with an expression of puzzled questioning.]

The SAINT. What am I asked to see? There is nothing save the spray of the waterfall swaying in the breeze of evening.

The WOMAN WORLDLY WISE. But there is more behind . . .

The SINNER (*with his hand on his wound, yet in a tone of triumph*). Ha! evil-minded hag! See now that ignorance and innocence are not the same!

The WOMAN WORLDLY WISE (*to the* SAINT). But can

you not hear, then, poor fool? The drunken shouts, the
ribald oaths, the blasphemous — Ah (*exultingly*), in *my*
day, I knew them all, and more!

The SAINT (*with her hand upon the rope of her bell*).   I
hear only your words, which have no meaning for me,
and the tones of my own bell, which never fails to sound
at the vesper hour.

The WOMAN WORLDLY WISE. That bell! — that tiresome, hateful bell! Stop it; what meaning does it hold?
What good has it ever done?

[The HERMIT emerges from the forest and advances
slowly, leaning on his staff.]

The HERMIT. One good at least: it has guided me to
this spot.

The SINNER. Are *you* come to tell, too, more than
should be known?

The HERMIT. I know your errand and your hope.
You seek redemption. I would help you to it. Why did
you pass me by to halt at this deceitful place? You
should have remained with me, sharing my seclusion and
meditation.

The SINNER. I can meditate anywhere at all. I must,
indeed; I have no choice. And as for seclusion, is yours,
on your lower level, more perfect than this?

The HERMIT. But the companionship of woman-
kind . . .

The SINNER. My salvation shall be worked out amidst
all the elements that make up this present world.

The WOMAN WORLDLY WISE. Ay, and the world
means knowledge of the world. You are for *me* — believe
it. Leave this forceless old man; leave this untutored

child. I know herbs; I can heal your wound upon the instant . . .

The SINNER. Hush, temptress! The wound you see is only one of many.

[The early moon has risen. Its beams lie slantingly upon the waterfall and weave a rainbow from its spray. The swans have sought their beds along the sedgy shores of the pool, and the lambs are folded in the shelter of a wide-spreading tree.

Suddenly the IGNORAMUS, holding a half-tamed lion in leash, comes bounding down the mountain-side. In his belt he carries a knife and a flower indescribably brilliant and pungent. He stands regarding the group before him with an expression of vacant good-nature.]

The SINNER. Who is this youth?

The HERMIT. I know him. I have seen him once before, and have heard of him oftener than that. I have heard, indeed, that he bears within him the saving grace of innocence — that he vibrates with the heavenly power of one who is completely attuned to nature.

The SINNER (*fretfully*). Why should he stand here gaping at nothing? If he is a fount of harmony, let him string my harp anew and play upon it.

The HERMIT (*to the* IGNORAMUS, *toward whom he extends the harp*). Can you play upon this? (*The* IGNORAMUS *nods with a bright confidence.*)

The SINNER. Can you tune it? (*The* IGNORAMUS *nods as before.*) Then let him have it.

[The IGNORAMUS snatches the harp with a glad curiosity. Within a moment he has snapped its strings, crushed

its frame, and has thrown its fragments, with a chuckle of
fond delight and of challenged approval, upon the ground.]

The SINNER. He is a fool.

The WOMAN WORLDLY WISE. He has better powers
than those of his hands. He has stronger forces within
his belt — did he but know how to employ them.

The HERMIT. The knife?

The WOMAN WORLDLY WISE. And the flower. Have
you not noticed its flaming petals? Have you not per-
ceived its pungent perfume? (*To the* SINNER.) One
touch from that blossom would heal your wound. Shall I
snatch it?

The SINNER (*groaning in pain and vexation*). I wish no
aid either from you or yours.

The WOMAN WORLDLY WISE. He is naught of mine —
though I might easily make him so. But I can cure you
without his help. Let me do it.

The SINNER. Only innocence can redeem me.

The HERMIT. *He* is innocent.

The SINNER. You mistake. He is ignorant.

The WOMAN WORLDLY WISE (*pointing to the* SAINT).
She is ignorant.

The SINNER. You mistake again. She is innocent.

The HERMIT. You are stubborn. Turn away from this
fatal preference. At least defend your own logic.

The SINNER. In man innocence is mere ignorance; in
woman ignorance is but innocence. Nothing is simpler.
I have to choose between the ignorance of man and the
innocence of woman, and I have made my choice.

[The IGNORAMUS, who has been standing in smiling
doubt, suddenly draws his knife, seizes one of the lambs,

slits its throat, and throws its body to the lion.   The lion
retires with its booty within the dark edge of the wood.]

The SAINT (*with a faint cry*). My lamb!

The SINNER (*with a shout of helpless rage*).   Her lamb!
her lamb! What do you mean, O blundering fool?

The WOMAN WORLDLY WISE. The lamb is mine.   This
youth is indeed a fool.   But (*to the* SINNER) what is one
lamb to you?—you who have rent your scores!

The HERMIT. He is a fool, yes; a blunderer, no.   There
is more power, more grace, more salvation in his simple
folly than in all our wisdom.   (*The* IGNORAMUS *offers an
inane smile alike to praise and to blame*.)

The SINNER. Why am I to believe that?

The HERMIT. Because I say so.

The SINNER. I will not believe you.   I will not be aided
by you.   Nor by *his* ignorance.   Nor by *her* knowledge.

The WOMAN WORLDLY WISE. What then shall save
you?

The SINNER. This maiden's innocence.

The WOMAN WORLDLY WISE. Then she shall be innocent no longer.   For she shall — know.   Look! (*She
waves her hand toward the waterfall*.)   But it is not I, remember, who call up this vision; that is the work of your
own guilty heart and gnawing conscience.   Look, all of
you!

[BALLET.—The veil of the waterfall parts once more
and shows the cavern aflame with an unearthly light and
a-swarm with many madly-swirling figures.   Lines of stag-
gering bacchantes weave to and fro, to the piercing notes
of reeds and viols and to the delicate tingle and clang of
brasses.— A vast burning heart bursts asunder, and TEMP-

TATION herself, robed in clamorous scarlet and crowned with flaring flames, comes whirling to the fore.]

The WOMAN WORLDLY WISE (*to the* SINNER). Do you see it?

The SINNER. In part. But there is a great canopied throne which still rests in shadow. Who sits upon it?

The WOMAN WORLDLY WISE. The Master of the Revels. You shall see his face in good time.

[The HERMIT, meanwhile, sunk on his knees and with his hands pressed against his eyes, tremblingly strives to stammer out a prayer. The IGNORAMUS, starting forward with a fierce joy dawning upon his face, emits inarticulate cries of rapture at the spectacle, and in anticipation of other spectacles yet to succeed. The SAINT glances from one to another of the group with an air of plaintive questioning.]

The WOMAN WORLDLY WISE. Enough of that. Let other revels follow.

[The plants that fringe and frame the waterfall now expand into gigantic blooms of amazing brilliancy; their crinkled edges flame with hell-fire. Within the cavern, bands of fauns and satyrs, accompanied by bassoons and cymbals, sweep in giddy circles round a whited sepulcher. The sepulcher is suddenly rent in twain, and PERDITION, powdered with gold and clad in voluminous swirls of floating black gauze, comes reeling through their ranks. Her eyes flash and scintillate with exultant terrors; and the HERMIT, trembling in every limb, falls half prostrate on the ground, while the IGNORAMUS, with a wild shout of rapture, snatches the blossom from his belt and throws it at her feet.]

The WOMAN WORLDLY WISE. Aha! an apt pupil, indeed! There is much for me to teach him, and he will learn it — oh, he will learn it!

The SINNER. You shall not have him.

The WOMAN WORLDLY WISE. How can you save him? You have yet to save yourself.

The SAINT. You are an evil woman. I have long feared so. (*She gropes for the rope of her bell, but cannot find it in the dark.*)

[Pas de Deux.— Through the floor rise RUINATION and DAMNATION (a man among women) decked in desperate convolutions of red and black and yellow. They swirl and swing and swoon, before a shifting array of imps and devils. A fierce light beats upon their gyrations, but the throne behind them still remains in shadow.]

The SINNER. Again I ask—Who sits upon that throne?

The WOMAN WORLDLY WISE. You shall know in good time. (*To the* SAINT.) Look, girl; here are things to see that you have never seen before.

The SAINT. My eyes are not your eyes. (*She folds her hands and looks up at the stars that shine above the mountain-tops.*)

[Pas Seul by the prima assoluta, TORMENT-EVERLAST-ING. She is clothed in the coruscations of clear combustion, all crisp and crinkling and crimson. To the screams of violins, the shrieks of trumpets and the shivers of drums she trips and twists with an unconquerable and inexhaus-

tible agility through ranks and rows of quivering flames;
her limbs are distorted by tendons racked and strained,
and her face is wreathed with an endless succession of
agonizing smiles. The HERMIT, with his hands writhing
in a locked twist, lies prostrate upon the chapel steps, while
the IGNORAMUS is seen madly floundering through the pool
toward the cavern.]

The SINNER. But who sits in the shadow on that throne?
The WOMAN WORLDLY WISE. The time has come for
you to know.

[The inner stage is invaded by a flood of nymphs, sirens,
bacchantes, satyrs, amoretti, imps and demons. They
presently flow to right and left in two great waves, and
leave an open way up to the steps that rise to the canopied
seat.]

The WOMAN WORLDLY WISE. It is *you* who sit upon
that throne.
The SINNER. You lie. I am not seated there. You
cannot place me there. You cannot show me there.
The WOMAN WORLDLY WISE. I shall.
The SINNER (*now standing close beside the* SAINT). Try,
then! — You cannot.
The WOMAN WORLDLY WISE (*to the* SAINT). Look, girl.
You have seen his associates. Now I will show you the
man himself in the midst of them.
The SAINT. I do not know what you mean. I see only
what the evening has often brought me: the rainbow above
my waterfall and the spray that sparkles upon its shrubs
and vines.
The WOMAN WORLDLY WISE. You know more than you

will confess.   Well, then, if you will not look, only listen.
If you will not listen, only smell.   Have you no nose for
sulphur, for brimstone, for the fumes of the Pit?

The SAINT. Your presence is the only stench.

The WOMAN WORLDLY WISE. Ha!   You dare to — ?

The SINNER. Peace, hag!   You boast your knowledge:
learn at last to recognize the truth when spoken.

The WOMAN WORLDLY WISE. But she shall see one
thing: she shall see you upon that throne.   Look!

[The throne is suddenly illumined.   It is empty.   The
WOMAN, with a shriek of rage and mortification, falls half
fainting to the ground.]

The SAINT. I think that she is mad.   I think the evil
spirits possess her.   I will ring my bell.

[She rings it.   The throng within the cavern vanishes.
The rainbow again spans the waterfall, and in its spray the
IGNORAMUS, beslimed with mud and torn by the jagged
rocks, is seen in a gasping struggle for his life.]

The SINNER (*taking the hand of the* SAINT). Come, let
us leave this place; let us ascend to the spring.   You can
no longer live here alone — you would be no safer than
your swans and your lambs.   Your touch strengthens me;
we will make the ascent together.   Where lies the path?

The SAINT. There; on the other bank of the stream.

The SINNER. How shall we cross to it?

The HERMIT (*rising on his elbows*). Let *me* save you.

The WOMAN WORLDLY WISE (*struggling to her feet*).
Let *me* save you.

The IGNORAMUS (*in a vain repetition, as he drags himself to land*). Let *me* save you.

The SINNER. Away with you, one and all! I place no trust in trembling feebleness, in floundering ignorance, in knowledge of worldly evil. I have chosen my guide.

The WOMAN WORLDLY WISE. Follow her — a guide indeed! One with neither sense nor senses! Yet you trust her to lead you to peace and to paradise!

The SINNER (*to the* SAINT). How do we cross to the other bank? Must we wade through the pool?

The SAINT. No.

The SINNER. Must we pass through the cavern?

The SAINT. I know of no cavern.

The SINNER. Then . . .

The SAINT. We shall cross over on the rainbow.

The SINNER. The rainbow? That may be done, perhaps — but by the gods alone.

The SAINT. We are become gods — for we have the knowledge of good and of evil.

The SINNER (*with a flush*). Yes, we possess — between us — the knowledge of all evil and of all good.

The SAINT. Come, give me your hand.

[They pass over on the rainbow and take in the moonlight the upward path. The Three who remain behind slink back with downcast mien into the dark forest.]

ON THE WHIRLWIND

THE AVES MINH

ON THE WHIRLWIND.

"Rides on the whirlwind and directs the storm."

PERSONS.

The MASTER.	The MILLIONAIRE.
His PUPIL.	A GIRL, his Daughter.
A Young LIEUTENANT.	An Old PRESSMAN.

A workshop in the midst of a vast city and high above it. Wide windows command the roofs that shelter a million people and the harbor to which has come for generations the tribute of a world. A high wind sweeps freely round; it causes the defiant flaunting of a myriad flags — but the same flag always, and it will bring at intervals great swirling clouds of dun and pungent smoke. Outside the harbor one sees an aggregation of enormous ironclads, whose flag is not the flag above the roofs all round about: the clouds of smoke, too, will come from that same quarter, for the smoke is to be the smoke of battle.

The room is cumbered with the varied apparatus of science, and through every window the air is seen to be cut by the black lines of multitudes of wires that radiate to every point of the compass.

The MASTER, a grave, self-absorbed man of thirty-five, stands looking out at one of the windows. No one can be sure of what he sees, or of his seeing anything at all; it can only be certain that his hands, with corded veins and half-purpled nails, are strained in a motionless and vise-like grip behind his back.

———

The PUPIL (*a young fellow of twenty*). They have called for a million more men.

The LIEUTENANT (*his arm in a sling*). I am a man, and I have answered a call already.

The PUPIL. And for a thousand millions of money.

The MILLIONAIRE (*his hand in his pocket*). I have my millions and I have given freely.

The LIEUTENANT. The men are forthcoming — we are populous.

The MILLIONAIRE. And the millions — we are rich.

The PUPIL. We have them already — men and money alike.

The GIRL. Already?

The PUPIL. Yes; they are here. The million men stand looking out of that window. The millions of money are held between those hands.

[From the sea there comes suddenly a dull roar; the battle-ships are at once half-lost in their own smoke. The MASTER gives a quick start.]

The LIEUTENANT. The hour has struck. They are doing what they have threatened.

The GIRL. Who could have believed that they would do it? — that they would dare to do it? Can so many efforts, so many sacrifices, all go in vain?

The MILLIONAIRE (*to the* MASTER). Wake, man; this is your moment! Every second of delay means untold loss and suffering.

The PUPIL. Trust him. You hear too plainly the cries

and blows that assail our outer door.   The populace in the streets below call up to the prophets on the landing-stage; and the prophet-scribes, with tablet and stylus, appeal to the priests; but let not these unduly importune the god himself.   He will act of his own will, at his own time, in his own way.   Let them go on clamoring for the miracle; it will be wrought in due course.

[A shell from the sea flies in a long curve through the air and explodes disastrously not half a mile away.   There is a feeble response from shore.   And from the roofs of the city, black with people, thousands of invoking arms and thousands of imploring voices are sent upward to the MASTER's tower.]

The MILLIONAIRE. Look! The time is come! No more delay!

The LIEUTENANT. Come, do the deed quickly — in recognition of our help.

The GIRL. And in justification of our faith.

The MILLIONAIRE. Remember the thousands that our vaults have yielded up to you.

The LIEUTENANT. Remember the assistance that my fellow officers have rendered you.

The MASTER. It is a dreadful thing to do.   There are ten thousand of them, if there are twenty.

The MILLIONAIRE. Is it worse for one man to slay ten thousand than for ten thousand to slay a million and to lay their city in ruins?

The LIEUTENANT. The triumph is to be yours, not theirs: enjoy it.

The MASTER. My triumph consists not in doing, but in knowing that I *can* do. (*He turns away again.*)

The MILLIONAIRE. You must do it — and at once. Lives and property are in danger. I command you. (*He lays an eager hand upon the* MASTER'S *arm.*)

The PUPIL (*sweeping his hand aside*). Learn your place! Is this the way you can treat a genius? — a man who is able to bring the unseen to our eyes, the unheard to our ears, who can weigh what no one else can even lay hold upon — a man who has wrenched the hidden forces from the earth and the air, and has learned how to drag forth mysterious powers from the deep bosom of the sea itself!

The MILLIONAIRE. So you tell us; so you have told us many times within the last fortnight. Now let him do it.

The LIEUTENANT. Let *me* do it. (*He rushes impulsively across to a table in the midst of whose tangle of wires and plates and tubes there rests a broad board set thick with levers, knobs and keys.*) Which is the one?

The PUPIL. Hands off! Do you know what you might do?

The LIEUTENANT. Do? Something—anything; this is the time, if ever.

The PUPIL. You have done something already; let that suffice.

The GIRL. Indeed he has. We have not found him satisfied to sit in safety far above the city. He has gone down like a man. He has taken his sword in hand —

The PUPIL. Yes, yes; I know. He has mounted upon the breastwork, he has shouted, he has waved his blade; while I, poor coward, have done nothing more worthy than to fill jars and to couple wires. To wave and shout upon a breastwork,—that is gallant, that is picturesque, that is exhilarating. But what, in the end, have you thousands of wavers and shouters accomplished?

The GIRL. They have done their best.

The MASTER (*turning slowly*). Their best, Oswald. Even if one's best amounts to nothing, still it is one's best and should have praise as such.

The LIEUTENANT. Thanks for that generous concession!

The MILLIONAIRE (*looking through his glass*). They are preparing to follow up the attack. Their decks swarm with jaunty officers all careless of danger; the men aloft laugh across from crow's-nest to crow's-nest and wave their hands in jest . . . ! (*Throws down his glass.*) Act, man; act!

[Another dull roar is heard, and again a great smoke-cloud obscures the harbor. The wind sweeps over the populous roofs at a wilder pace and bears the fumes of battle with it. The flags below flaunt with a fiercer defiance, but one of them, not a furlong distant, now flaps all torn and shredded in the gale. A shell strikes the proud building above which it rises.]

The MILLIONAIRE. Man, man, are you benumbed? That building is mine — mine! If you care nothing for the city, at least do something for the citizen whose money has made all your experiments and investigations possible. Oh, where are the fortresses that we should have built? where are the ships that we should have floated? Far better to have surrendered — to have paid a ransom . . . ! Quick, quick! touch the key!

The MASTER. The time is approaching. But they must be made to understand who has saved them, and how, and from what. I look for no other return.

The GIRL. You can look for the fervent gratitude of a great country.

The LIEUTENANT. And for all the honors that this magnificent city can bestow.

The MILLIONAIRE. And for money beyond your utmost needs.

The PUPIL. And for a fame that can never die.

The MASTER (*to the* PUPIL, *with a melancholy smile which ignores the others*). You may be right, Oswald. For that are we poets.

[A wild tumult of yells ascends from the street. And there is a medley of scuffles and cries on the other side of the workshop door.]

The PUPIL. Again the crowd calls up to the prophets, and the prophets — true or false — pass on the word. (*To the* MASTER.) Let us meet their demand.

The MILLIONAIRE. If you can, if you can!— You cannot! My hope, my trust, my money, all gone for naught! My property destroyed before my very eyes!— they know that I have helped to make you possible!

The PUPIL (*ironically*). Your fame is world-wide, even now! What that we may do could make it wider?

The MASTER. Hush, Oswald. (*He advances toward the table and places his hand upon one of the keys. Then, pausing, he turns to the* GIRL *with a touch of timid and awkward gallantry.*) Would *you* like to do it?

The PUPIL (*hastening to his side and speaking in a low, hurried tone*). What! you, the great mind of the age, yield up such a moment to a mere casual bystander! The end crowns the work; the work crowns you; you should place the crown upon your own head.

The MASTER (*with an embarrassed smile*). Hardly a casual bystander, Oswald; she has been here every day for a fortnight, and I had thought to recognize her interest. We must try to bear in mind that part of the world which lies outside of science — we are but too likely to forget it.

The PUPIL. But it shall never forget us.

The MASTER (*aloud, to the* GIRL). Come, will you press the key?

[The GIRL scans the harbor; then she looks into the MASTER's face and silently shrinks away.]

The MASTER (*to himself*). I knew it! I have suspected it for days.— Yet I am a human being, after all.

The LIEUTENANT. It is an awful thing, but it must be done. It is no woman's work — let *me* do it.

[The GIRL looks at him with a startled admiration; then she lays a detaining hand upon his arm.]

The MILLIONAIRE. Then let me do it; no one, I am sure, has better earned the right —

The PUPIL. We do not deny the right to bravery, nor even to beauty; but the right of mere — *I* will do it.

The MASTER. Hush, Oswald. (*His hand again advances toward the keyboard.*)

[Renewed disorder outside the door. Cries of " Hold him back!" "No favor must be shown!" "He cannot enter unless we enter too!" The PRESSMAN precipitates himself into the room, with torn clothes and bleeding face.]

The PRESSMAN (*calling back*). It is as a friend that I am admitted; I am not meaning to take an unfair advantage.

[He slams the door and braces himself against it. The
PUPIL hastens to strengthen his resistance.]

The PUPIL. How did you dare do this?

The PRESSMAN. Bar the door — quick, quick! They
would pull me to pieces. — My key, my key! — where is
it? where have I dropped it?

The PUPIL. On this side of the door, I hope. But here
is mine.

The PRESSMAN (*recovering his breath, to the* MASTER).
Why this delay? The whole town is in a frenzy, a panic.
— What! you have tried and failed? Failed! — my God,
my God!

The PUPIL. We have not failed. We have not tried.

The PRESSMAN. Then try, in Heaven's name! Within
an hour the city will be a mere heap of smoking ruin, and
those of us who are left alive will be a mass of pitiful beg-
gars preying upon one another for the means of daily life.
Act, man; act! A moment's delay may mean your own
ruin and death. You little know the temper of the crowd
I fought my way through up your stairs. Act; you are
our only hope.

The MASTER. The only hope should be beyond rough
handling.

The PRESSMAN. Then haste to put it there. Come,
what is the thing to be done? (*He advances toward the
keyboard.*) If no one else will do it, let me do it.

The PUPIL (*pinning him in his arms and throwing him
back*). What presumption! What insolence! We forge
the sword and you would show us how to wield it!

[Another cannonade from the sea. A shell explodes
within a hundred yards of the MASTER's tower and tears

to sudden tatters the flag that strains in the gale from his window-ledge.]

The MILLIONAIRE. They know, they know! I *told* you that they knew!

The PUPIL. We shine by your light.— But act, my master; act.

[The MASTER, standing at his table with a drooping head, takes a deep reluctant breath and applies a long slow pressure to one of the keys. There is a vast and instantaneous response. He remains standing in an unaltered attitude, but the others, hastening to the window, see what no man has ever seen before, and hear what no man has ever heard. New forces have been summoned from the water and from the air and find themselves for the first time face to face in the service of man. The darkened sky seems full of vast gleaming scimitars; the sea splits widely into a great yawning chasm; the land rocks, and immeasurable clouds compounded of smoke and of spray and of new things yet without a name reel madly over the town and past the tower: for the elements of the elements have been loosed at last, and in a wider way than one has ever dared to dream the work of creation has been undone.]

The PUPIL (*exultingly, though nothing can yet be distinguished within the area where the cloud and the noise have alike been generated*). The millions of men and the thousand millions of money.

The GIRL (*dazed*). What have they done?

The PUPIL (*perversely*). Nothing.

The GIRL (*trying to look toward the* MASTER). What has *he* done?

The MASTER (*immovable, with eyes still downcast*). What was necessary.

The MILLIONAIRE (*struggling to master his own awe*). Why did you wait so long?

The MASTER. The quarrel was hardly mine. What, to one who would search out the very life-essence of the globe, are the wrangles of the poor insects that swarm upon its surface?

The PRESSMAN. That was not your reason. Why did you wait so long?

The MASTER. That I might secure the completest expression of our city's thanks. How better do this than to let the people feel that from which I was about to deliver them?

The PUPIL. Master, you do yourself an injustice. Tell us the real reason. Why did you wait so long?

[The MASTER raises his eyes for the first time and looks toward the GIRL. She, all a-tremble, refuses to meet his gaze. Instead, she looks out toward the sea, from which the great cloud is lifting and blowing away. She sees only a mass of rolling billows upon which no single vestige of human life or of human craft is visible. With an hysterical shudder she clasps her hands across her eyes.]

The GIRL. Take me away! Take me away from this horrible place! Take me away from the presence of this terrible man!

[The MASTER drops his head sadly. At the same time a wild shout of triumph rises from the roofs and from the streets, and a thousand feet are heard to be swarming up the stairs.]

The GIRL (*with a mounting fear*). They are coming! Take me away!

The PRESSMAN. I am the only one who has anything to fear!

The MASTER (*without looking up*). The private door, Oswald. There is no leaving by the other way.

[The GIRL, accompanied by her Father and the LIEU-TENANT, retires through a small door on the other side.]

The PRESSMAN. Sir, you have done a great thing.

The PUPIL. He has done the greatest thing. And he is sure of honor and wealth to the end of his days, and of fame far beyond that!

The PRESSMAN. They will pour riches upon you; they will prepare illuminations for you; they will raise statues to you.

[The MASTER smiles a melancholy and ironical smile.]

The PUPIL. He shall not be honored merely; he shall be worshiped. He need not go from among us to be apotheosized; he is a god already.

The PRESSMAN. What is the meaning of that smile? Do you think otherwise?

The MASTER. Yes.

The PRESSMAN. Are you thinking that — that the rewards of the world follow their own peculiar courses, and that — that he who confers a benefit upon everybody may get the thanks of nobody?

The PUPIL. How can you say that here and now?

The MASTER. Perhaps.

The PRESSMAN. Are you thinking, too, that you are not precisely a part of the established order, and that he who serves it, no less than he who amuses it, is likely one day to be thrown thanklessly aside?

The PUPIL. How can you preach so shameful a doctrine? How can you show yourself so merciless a cynic?

The MASTER. Possibly.

The PRESSMAN. Are you thinking that one may achieve the great new thing and yet bring himself no nearer to humanity and to human sympathies?

The PUPIL. That is not true! That cannot be true!

The MASTER (*glancing sidewise toward the private door*). That *is* true.

[The MILLIONAIRE and the LIEUTENANT appear, leading back the GIRL from the inner room.]

The LIEUTENANT. There is no escape. The crowd is as great on one side as on the other.

The MASTER (*advancing toward the* GIRL). There is no need of escape. You are perfectly safe here. (*The* GIRL *shrinks back.*)

The PUPIL (*indignantly*). Is this the way you can treat a man who is a genius,— who is almost a god?

The GIRL (*upon the verge of hysterics, as she clutches the* LIEUTENANT's *arm*). He may be a god; or he may be a monster. But he is not a man.

The PUPIL. He is more than a man.

The GIRL. He may be more than a man; or less than a man; or more and less both. But —

The PRESSMAN. Truly, man is not an intellectual being,

but an emotional being. And woman the same. How many more are there who would pass by the gray matter in one unique brain for the red fluid that pulses from any one of a hundred commonplace hearts!

The GIRL. I can understand—admire—love the man who bravely opposes his own body to those of his fellows; but what can I have save dread for the big, bloodless intelligence that sits aloft and calmly deals out death to ten thousand of his own kind . . . ?

The MASTER. (*sadly*). You see.

The PRESSMAN. I see. He who rides upon the whirlwind must ride alone.

The PUPIL. You shall not ride alone, dear Master. I shall have wings to follow you.

[The sound of a key is heard in the outer door, and the scuffling and struggling is renewed.]

The PRESSMAN. My key!—they have found it!

The MASTER. The whirlwind is upon us at last. (*To the* PRESSMAN.) I should not advise *you* to try to ride upon it!

The PUPIL. But *I* shall remain with you.

The PRESSMAN (*retiring, with the others, to the inner room*). They will devastate you like a cloud of locusts . . .

The MASTER. An idle interruption : the empty glory of an hour!

[The MASTER and his PUPIL remain there alone, to oppose the wreckage threatened by a pressing and enthusiastic populace.]

3

THE LOVE OF LOVE

THE LOVE OF LOVE.

PERSONS.

The NOBLE SPINSTER.
The GIRL'S FATHER.
The GIRL'S MOTHER.
The GIRL'S UNCLE.
Others of her Family.
The GIRL'S BETROTHED.
The YOUTH'S FATHER.

The YOUTH'S MOTHER.
Others of his Family.
The INTENDANT of the Monument.
A Band of Sailors.
A Train of Servants and Attendants.

A hilltop. A white marble wall, before which is drawn
up an inexorable array of Doric columns. In the middle
of the wall is a single doorway, which leads to darkness
save for the occasional reflection of red flames from within. On either side of the doorway there stands a burned-
out brazen funeral torch, and under the colonnade, as well
as on the steps which rise to it, are stationed several black-
draped groups that look out toward the horizon-line of the
sea. They are waiting. It is evening, and above the
tops of the cypress-trees which lead, in a long avenue, up
to the foot of the Monument the stars are shining — shining coldly, serenely, patiently, impersonally: they do not
care — they have seen too much. They give no heed to
the Monument, nor to the convent-isle that whitens in
their light a league from shore.

The GIRL'S MOTHER (*moaningly, as the flames once more light up the doorway*). How long? How long?

The GIRL'S FATHER (*who carries a rich golden urn in his hand*). Courage, courage. All will be over soon.

The YOUTH'S MOTHER (*on the other side of the doorway*). Let them learn that all are equal here.

The YOUTH'S FATHER (*who holds a plain earthen urn within the hollow of his arm*). Let them learn what the lowly have to suffer. Let them learn how long an hour may be.

The YOUTH'S MOTHER. An hour? One only? Two, rather; three. The torches have died out and the stars have come. I can stand here no longer. I shall drop from fatigue.

The YOUTH'S FATHER. Drop? Before *them?* You will stand here as you have stood, and you will stand till the end.

The YOUTH'S MOTHER. Till the end? There will be no end, I think.— See; the flush upon the doorway once more!

The YOUTH'S FATHER. Yes; but fainter. The flames are dying out. The ashes will soon be cold.

The YOUTH'S MOTHER. The ashes! the ashes!—Set down your urn; it is heavy, heavy, heavy.

The YOUTH'S FATHER. I will hold mine as long as they hold theirs.

The YOUTH'S MOTHER. But ours is heavier.

The YOUTH'S FATHER. So is our lot.

The YOUTH'S MOTHER. While theirs is richer.

The YOUTH'S FATHER. So are their lives.

The YOUTH'S MOTHER. It is we who have made them so.

The YOUTH'S FATHER. We have given them the best we had. And what, in return—?

The YOUTH'S MOTHER. Hush, hush! Their loss is no less than ours.

[The breeze stirs the tree-tops; it has rippled hillward over the sea.]

The GIRL'S MOTHER (*to the* FATHER, *who is intently gazing waterward*). What do you see? My eyes are too dull and weak for sight.

The GIRL'S FATHER. I see a white spot upon the water.

The GIRL'S MOTHER. It is the convent. I have often seen their island from here—and often heard their bell. I hear a bell now.

The GIRL'S FATHER. It is not the convent. What I see is moving—is moving over the water. It is a sail. I hear no bell.

The GIRL'S MOTHER. A sail? No, no; do not say a sail! Turn round, I beg you. Do not look longer at that cruel sea!

The GIRL'S FATHER. I hear no bell.

The GIRL'S MOTHER. But *I* hear one. A bell should be heard at such a time as this. Some one should ring a bell. Some one should ring the convent bell. Some one *is* ringing it. I hear it—I am sure I hear it.

The GIRL'S FATHER (*turning again toward the sea*). There is a sail. I see it plainly now.

The GIRL'S MOTHER. I see no sail. But there is a bell. I hear it plainly now.

The GIRL'S FATHER. I hear it too, I think. But it is not the convent bell. This is weaker, yet nearer. I think the sailors are ringing it.

The GIRL'S MOTHER. The sailors! Let us not speak of sailors!

The GIRL'S FATHER. Yes, there are sailors. I see them.

The GIRL'S MOTHER (*turning away*). Where do they come from?

The GIRL'S FATHER. Who can tell?

The GIRL'S MOTHER. Where are they going?

The GIRL'S FATHER. They are coming here.

The GIRL'S MOTHER. And their bell is tolling — tolling . . .

The GIRL'S FATHER. The hour?

The GIRL'S MOTHER. It is tolling — tolling . . .

[A small ship makes its way landward. Both masts carry full sail, and a white-robed figure waves greeting from the prow.]

The GIRL'S BETROTHED (*to her* FATHER). Let me hold the urn. It is too heavy for you.

The GIRL'S MOTHER. It is lighter than our grief.

The GIRL'S BETROTHED (*taking the urn from her* FATHER). Should your sister have known of this?

The GIRL'S FATHER. What — Constantia? No; she does well where she is.

The GIRL'S MOTHER. She has given up the world. She has her fasts, her prayers, her vigils.

The GIRL'S UNCLE. She dwells on the island. She will pray us all to Heaven.

The GIRL'S FATHER. She has renounced the world — and her kindred with it.

The GIRL'S MOTHER. Much has happened that she has never known.

The GIRL'S FATHER. Much is to happen that she will never know.

The GIRL'S UNCLE. She has the sea, the sky, the stars.

The GIRL'S FATHER. She has her books, and her beads, and her bells.

The GIRL'S GRANDMOTHER. She has her thoughts. And her memories . . .

The GIRL'S FATHER. She has no memories. She has no past.

The GIRL'S UNCLE. She has the future. She will be abbess in good time, and will pray us all to Heaven.

The GIRL'S FATHER. With her books, and her beads, and her bells.

The GIRL'S MOTHER. Her bells! — I hear one of them now.

The GIRL'S FATHER. It is not the nuns who are ringing that bell; it is the sailors.

The GIRL'S UNCLE. But why do they do it?

The GIRL'S GRANDFATHER. And why do they ring so loud and so long and so unceasingly? Even I can hear it.

The GIRL'S MOTHER. And who has told them to do it? And who stands over them to make sure that they never cease?

[The sound of a prow crunching on the shingle of the shore. The last faint glow illumines the lintel of the doorway. The breeze freshens; it is still from the sea.]

The YOUTH'S FATHER. Ha! the sailors!

The YOUTH'S YOUNGER BROTHER. Yes, yes; I recognize their voices.

The YOUTH'S MOTHER. The sailors, yes. But to-day there is one sailor the less.

The YOUTH'S FATHER. Who was standing at the prow?

The YOUTH's SISTER. Some one all in white.

The YOUTH's BROTHER. But none of our sailors dress
in white.

The YOUTH's MOTHER. It was a woman. I know it
was a woman.

The YOUTH's FATHER. Perhaps.— I trust our men will
follow.   They should be here — it is right that his com-
panions should be here.

The YOUTH's AUNT (*bitterly*). True; we are not many.
They (*pointing athwart the doorway*) have their hundreds.

[The INTENDANT appears in the doorway of the Monument.]

The INTENDANT (*to the* GIRL's FATHER). Is the urn
ready?

The YOUTH's FATHER. They come before us, even
here.

The YOUTH's MOTHER. As everywhere.

The YOUTH's BROTHER. The rich go before the poor.

The YOUTH's SISTER. The haughty before the humble.

The GIRL's FATHER (*advancing with his urn*). Yes, it
is ready.

The YOUTH's FATHER (*also advancing*).   Yes, it is
ready.   It is ready — mine, too, I say.   Mine, mine,
mine!

The GIRL's FATHER. Back, back! What do you mean
by this?

The YOUTH's BROTHER. It is not we who should be
second here.

The YOUTH's MOTHER. Our urn is earthen, but rightly
should be of gold.

The INTENDANT. Peace, peace. There can be no dispute at such a time as this.

The GIRL'S UNCLE. Nor in such a place. Let them *know* the place. Let them know *their* place!

The YOUTH'S MOTHER. Oh, ingratitude! You are forgetting what you should remember!

The GIRL'S MOTHER. Oh, insolence! You are forgetting what always has been remembered!

[A figure in white appears at the lower end of the cypress-avenue and comes up rapidly, accompanied by the scuffling of many feet.]

The GIRL'S FATHER. What can it be? Who can be coming?

The INTENDANT. Who dare to break in thus on this solemnity?

The GIRL'S FATHER (*to his major-domo*). Go, take a dozen of my followers and check the tumult before it reaches us.

The YOUTH'S MOTHER. It is a woman. I said it was a woman.

The YOUTH'S FATHER. It is a woman. And our sailors are behind her.

The GIRL'S FATHER. It is a woman. It is my sister. It is Constantia's self!

[The NOBLE SPINSTER, in the full habit of a nun, and with damp and disheveled hair, arrives panting at the lowest of the marble steps.]

The SPINSTER (*mounting; the sailors remain behind*). And no one told me! No one sent me a single word by way of message!

The GIRL's FATHER. You here, Constantia? You absent from your convent?

The GIRL's UNCLE. You sailing the sea alone in the darkness of the night? For shame! for shame!

The GIRL's MOTHER. The woman is mad. She is mad. Mad.

The SPINSTER. And no one would have told me! No one would have told me!

The GIRL's FATHER. Why should we have told you?

The GIRL's MOTHER. You are out of the world — and well out of it, too.

The GIRL's UNCLE. There are many things that you cannot hope to know.

The GIRL's FATHER. Your niece is dead — yes. Even I might well be dead without your hearing of it. There are many things that you cannot hope to know.

The SPINSTER. But there are things that I can hope to know. There are things that I do know. For two evenings I saw no light — neither his nor hers. Then I did know. I knew something had befallen. I asked these sailors. And then I came.

The GIRL's MOTHER. Yes, she is mad. Mad.

The SPINSTER (*suddenly, as she glances at the young man beside the* GIRL's FATHER). Who is this?

The GIRL's FATHER. Our child's betrothed.

The SPINSTER (*with shrill laughter*). Our child's betrothed! And what is he carrying in his hand?

The GIRL's FATHER. The urn for her ashes.

The SPINSTER (*with shriller laughter*). The urn for her ashes! And why should *he* carry it? (*Suddenly.*) Where is *his*?

The GIRL's FATHER. His?

The GIRL's BETROTHED. Mine?

The SPINSTER. His, his! His, I say! My hero's—
my sailor's!

The YOUTH'S FATHER (*advancing*). Here it is.

The SPINSTER (*frantically*). Is this for him? This? For
him—for my hero? No, no; it is only of earth; the
other is of gold. His must be of gold too.

The YOUTH'S FATHER. I can provide nothing better
than this.

The SPINSTER. Then let the other be his. He shall have
nothing less than gold; for he was mine. Mine, I tell
you—mine!

The YOUTH'S MOTHER. Yours?

The SPINSTER. Yes, mine. For once I saved his life;—
just as he, not many hours past, would have saved hers.

The GIRL'S UNCLE. You saved his life, Constantia?
What can you mean?

The SPINSTER. I saved his life, I say! Ask these men.

The CAPTAIN OF THE SAILORS. It is true. His boat was
wrecked upon their coast, beneath the convent walls.

The SPINSTER. I nursed him. I saved him. I learned
his secret. He was mine, and I gave him up to her.

The GIRL'S MOTHER. His secret? You gave him up?
To whom?

The SPINSTER. To her—to your daughter.

The GIRL'S FATHER. This is unseemly.

The GIRL'S BETROTHED. This can never have been.

The SPINSTER (*to the* GIRL'S BETROTHED). I saved his
life. Whose life have you ever saved? Hers? Who
stood there pale and helpless, two days agone, when the
ship went down? He? Or you? No; do not try to
tell me—blush and be silent. I have heard. I know.

The GIRL'S BETROTHED (*stammeringly*). She is mad
indeed.

The SPINSTER. Yes, he told me all. I knew of his love and hers; she came to us on the island. How her beautiful eyes shone! — never did I see her happier.— And I came to know, as well, what the two lights meant. I came to know, I say. To know. Did *you* know? Did *any* of you know?

The GIRL'S FATHER. To know? The two lights? . . .

The SPINSTER. Yes. His in his cabin on the shore; hers in her turret on the hill.

The GIRL'S BETROTHED. This is impossible. This is shameful.

The SPINSTER. It is true. *You* are shameful. I know that too.

The GIRL'S UNCLE. Peace, Constantia.

The SPINSTER. When the ship pounded to pieces on the beach below, who braved the sea to save her? Who lost his life in the attempt? You? No; you are alive; her urn is in your hand.

The YOUTH'S MOTHER. There is such a thing as memory.

The YOUTH'S FATHER. There is such a thing as gratitude.

The SPINSTER. Yes, there were two lights, and one was hers. I saw it at midnight many a time and oft. There are other lights than the stars. There are other vigils than mine. There are other thoughts than those of the cloister. I know it — I am sure of it. Have you known these things too? But there are many things one cannot hope to know. Yes, that is true.

The GIRL'S UNCLE. Silence, Constantia! You forget yourself.

The SPINSTER. I do. And I forget other things. I am forgetting who stands here ready to receive her ashes. Not he, not he! Never! (*She tries to snatch the golden urn from the hands of the* GIRL'S BETROTHED.)

The INTENDANT. Time passes. The fires are out. The ashes are cold. Give me the urns.

The SPINSTER (*trying a second time*). The golden one must be his.

The GIRL'S FATHER. Never! (*He moves toward the door with his urn.*)

The SPINSTER. You shall not be first. *He* shall be first.

The GIRL'S UNCLE. By no means. We have always been first.

The GIRL'S FATHER. And must be first now.

The INTENDANT. Give me both.

[He receives the two urns at the same time from the hands of the two FATHERS and retires through the doorway.]

The CAPTAIN OF THE SAILORS (*looking aloft*). The wind is changing.

The SPINSTER (*clasping her hands over her streaming hair*). And freshening.

The CAPTAIN. It is blowing toward the sea.

The SPINSTER. It is blowing toward our island. It is blowing toward the convent.

The CAPTAIN. It will freshen still more. With every minute.

The SPINSTER. It sweeps this hilltop. Already it is able to carry everything over the waves — sound, smoke, dust, ashes . . .

[The INTENDANT appears in the doorway with an urn in each hand. The two families advance to receive them.]

The Spinster (*springing forward*). His ashes! And
hers! They should be mingled!

The Girl's Father. Never!

The Girl's Betrothed. Never such a degradation!

The Girl's Uncle. No more their ashes than their
blood.

The Youth's Father. Not less would be the dishonor
for me than for you.

The Spinster (*snatching at the covers of the two urns*).
Yes, yes; a thousand times yes! Or there is no right, no
justice, no love!

The Intendant. Back, woman; back!

The Youth's Mother. There *is* no right. There *is*
no justice.

The Spinster. But do not tell me there is no love.
There are many things one cannot know, but *that* . . .
Poor children, poor children!

[The Spinster wrenches the two urns from the hands
of the Intendant, and attempts to empty the contents of
the earthen one into the golden one. A sudden gust of
wind sweeps through the colonnade, and a bright beacon-
light flares on the topmost tower of the convent. The
Spinster, blinded by the blowing of her own hair, or by
the swirling ashes, drops both urns with a crash upon the
marble pavement. The wind sweeps the hilltop wildly
and makes for the open sea.]

The Youth's Mother. Woman, woman, what have
you done?

The Girl's Father. What have you done?

The Captain of the Sailors. What have you done?

The Spinster (*laughing wildly*). Ha, ha! The wind

blows straight to the island! I left my lattice wide open!
(*Seizing the* CAPTAIN's *arm.*) Come, come; they will be
waiting for me! They know the place! Let us return!
Let us return! Let us return!

[The SPINSTER, followed by her Sailors, runs rapidly
down the cypress-avenue. The launching of her ship is
heard above the protests and lamentations of those who
are left behind. The INTENDANT enters the Monument,
and shuts the door.]

AFTERGLOW

AFTERGLOW.

PERSONS.

The DRAMATIC POET.　　An OLD CRITIC.
His NIECE.　　THE LEADING LADY (retired).
The EX-MANAGER OF THE　Her SON.
　　COURT THEATER.　　A MAID-SERVANT.

A domestic interior in the environs of one of the Northern capitals. A bookcase full of pompous old volumes. A desk crammed with dusty and disordered papers. A floor-rug littered with journals from which excerpts have been made by hasty tearing or clipping. Present: the MAID-SERVANT, who has an idle duster in one hand and a packet of manuscript in the other.

———

The MAID-SERVANT (*considering the packet of manuscript*). How to bring it to his notice — that is the question. Shall I lay it on his desk and say it was brought by hand, or should I have fallen back upon the mails and have had it left by the postman? Shall it be the work of a lady of fortune and position, or that of a young poet whose only wish is to follow in the footsteps of the master? Which pages will be most likely to please him? Here is

the third act, for instance, where Pompilius leaves the
Forum :

> I go, my fellow-countrymen, I go;
> And proud the day for Rome when I return
> With a long train of captives . . .

Yes, yes; that does very well.   But there 's the fourth,
too, where Alymon and Julia are on the point of separation :

> Plead not, my love, you scarce know what you ask.
> Since that dread day when Priscus' raging horde
> Drove back our bands . . .

Ah, yes; I have written as *he* would have written.   He
must like it — must praise it.   But the question remains :
how bring it to his notice ?

[The street-door opens suddenly.   Enter, briskly, the
POET's NIECE, returned from a walk.   She advances di-
rectly toward the MAID-SERVANT.]

The NIECE. Give it to me, Lisbeth; give me Waldemar's letter.   I saw the postman leaving our door just as
I turned the corner.

The MAID-SERVANT. This is not Waldemar's letter—
it is something a good deal more valuable than that, I
hope !   There *is* no Waldemar's letter — nothing was left
but half a dozen more newspapers.   O, those newspapers!
— what are they all about ?

The NIECE. You are teasing me, Lisbeth.   This is one
of Waldemar's days and he has never failed to remember
me.   Where have you put it ?

The MAID-SERVANT (*snatching a letter from the corner of the* POET's *desk*).   Very well, then; this *is* one of his days, and he *has* remembered you.   (*She holds the letter behind her back.*)

The NIECE. Oh, Lisbeth, what were you meaning? To leave it upon my uncle's desk when you know that . . . ? What would he have said? — he who is so opposed to Waldemar (though he has never seen him), and to all of Waldemar's family.

The MAID-SERVANT. It has not been lying there two minutes; it would not have lain there two minutes longer. Have no fear of your uncle; he is still in the dark.   But oh, these Wednesday mornings, when I must be first, come what may, to answer the postman's rap!

The NIECE. Well, then, give it to me — come, come! Give it to me, like the good old soul that you are.

The MAID. Not so fast.   If I do all this for you, there is something that you must do for me.

The NIECE. What?

The MAID. You must bring this (*extending the manuscript*) to your uncle's notice.   You must get his attention for it; you must arouse his interest in it.

The NIECE. What is it?

The MAID. My play.

The NIECE. Your play, Lisbeth?   You have written a play?

The MAID. I have.

The NIECE (*taking the manuscript*). It is a — a tragedy?

The MAID. A Roman tragedy.

The NIECE. In four — no, in five acts.

The MAID. In five acts — five, of course.   The first act takes place on the Capitol; the second, in the ante-chamber of the Senate-house; the third, before the portals of —

The NIECE. Oh, Lisbeth, Lisbeth, you have succumbed at last! Twenty years in the atmosphere of tragedy — dusting it, shelving it, seeing it written, hearing it recited . . .

The MAID. Never mind. Take it; help it. Written by a woman of rank and fortune . . . too modest to let her name be known . . . Oh, well, say anything you think will serve.

The NIECE. I will. And now — Waldemar's letter. I must know what he thought of that book, and whether the flowers were fresh when they reached him.

The MAID. Take it.

The NIECE (*reading the letter*). "My darling Elsa: — I have but this moment received the sad intelligence — my poor, poor child."— Why, Lisbeth, what does this mean? What sad intelligence, pray? "By the merest accident . . . be sure that I will come at the earliest moment . . . . this sudden and terrible visitation . . . my mother's deepest sympathies . . . she will accompany me . . . the utmost haste . . . pray we may not be too late . . ." Oh, Lisbeth, what can he mean? I do not understand it at all. What dreadful thing has happened? Tell me, if you know, I beseech you!

The MAID. Nothing has happened, so far as I am aware.

The NIECE. Something *has* happened. Something must have happened. Where is my uncle?

The MAID. He is in his bedroom, shaving himself.

The NIECE. "This sudden and terrible visitation," he says. And his mother is coming, he adds. Why should his mother be coming?

The MAID. Let her come, if she likes; she is a fine enough old lady, as I remember her. When I was young,

how I used to sit and blubber over her in the gallery!
There was the woman to play my Julia! —

Nay, should'st thou doubt me, snatch thy naked blade,
And in this tender bosom plunge it deep! . . .

If he won't explain what the trouble is, perhaps she will.

The NIECE. Lisbeth, you are deceiving me — you are
holding something back.

The MAID. I am holding nothing back — except my
real name. I have deceived your uncle — steadily, for
the past month, or more — but I have never deceived you.
— See, he is coming. Control yourself; seem calm and
placid — or he may think you are the author yourself.
(*She glides out.*)

[Enter the DRAMATIC POET — a small, thin, sour and
discontented man. He falls straightway upon the morning's mail, regardless of his NIECE, who hovers in the back-
ground with her attention divided between her own letter
and LISBETH's manuscript.]

The POET. Twenty years of indifference, twenty years
of neglect! — such unworthy, such shameful treatment for
the greatest dramatic author of the age! The theater
closed against me; my name all but forgotten; my career
ending dingily in a disregarded suburb! — Well, what have
these creatures found to say of me? (*He removes the
wrapper from the first newspaper.*)

Yes, I have taken a decisive step, and I do not regret it.
To languish for twenty years unmentioned, unheeded —
it is too much. To find myself gliding toward the dark
shadow without the faintest ray of illumination that comes

from the afterglow of fame — the thought was not to be endured. I must go sometime, yes; but I could not bear to be snuffed out in silence.

I consider that I have done no wrong in myself starting the report of my serious illness and imminent death. No great man can hope for full appreciation until his footfall is close upon the dark verge; but when *all* appreciation is withheld — then extreme measures are justifiable. I will *not* pass away before my eyes are gladdened by one little belated flicker from the careless torch of fame. (*Cursory examination of newspaper.*)

Well? well? What do they say? Into what obscure corner have they tucked it? It is not here; it is not there! Can it be that no . . . ? Since so little can be hoped for at the best, I will not degrade myself by further search. (*He tramples the first journal under foot and opens a second.*)

First column, second column, third column; first page, second page — Ah! . . . Three lines; three lines — no more. " We learn that Leopold Heiberg, a dramatic author who once enjoyed a considerable repute, lies seriously ill at his house in Vorstadt. His recovery is doubtful." Ah! . . . *A* dramatic author! *A!* And — " considerable repute "! Did not rival managers compete for my plays? Did not ministers and councilors of state delight to honor me? Did not royalty itself pin decorations on my breast? Did not the king . . . ? (*He notes the presence of his* NIECE.) Elsa, open the bookcase and bring me the first volume of the Collected Works.— And — "his recovery is doubtful." Is there one word of solicitude? Is there one expression of regret? O shame! O shame!

No, no; not that edition. Bring me the tall quarto.— There! What does the first page say? Whose name heads the list of patrons? — Well, well; are not the letters big enough to read?

ELSA. They are. They say: His Most Gracious Majesty, Otto Frederick the Twelfth.

The POET. And what decoration did he bestow upon me?

ELSA. I know, I know: the Order of the Golden Gadfly.

The POET. And when I next appeared before the public — when " Polymedon in Paphlagonia " first saw the footlights — tell me, girl, were there odes, were there laurel wreaths, were there toasts and banquets? . . .

ELSA. There were — so I am told.

The POET. So you are told? Open that drawer. Yes — that one. What do you bring me?

ELSA. A laurel-wreath.

The POET. Of silver. With purple ribbons. And gold lettering. How does it read?

ELSA. You know, uncle; I know; we both know.

The POET. Lay it on my desk. And replace the book. — What have you in your hand? What have you been keeping there all this time?

ELSA. A — a letter; a manuscript, I mean.

The POET. A letter; a manuscript; of course it is a manuscript. — Ah, I have been fearing this. I am not so ignorant of all that has been passing. Is it from Waldemar Kronborg?

ELSA. See, uncle; a manuscript — truly. Left this morning by a lady — by a woman of fortune and position . . .

The POET. Never mind. I am thinking of *his* fortune and position — and family. Is the letter from him?

ELSA. Yes.

The POET. You must not see him; you must not think

of him.   I know the Kronborgs.   I know Gertrude Kronborg: never will I forgive her so long as I live.

ELSA. Oh, uncle, what has happened? Something dreadful, I know! Tell me, tell me!

The POET. Yes?   When?

ELSA. But lately.   I have just heard.

The POET. But lately?   That was years ago.— Well,
what is it?

ELSA. I do not know.— Oh, uncle, are you happy — are
you well?

The POET. Are you?

ELSA. Oh, uncle, you look so strange!·— you behave
so — so . . .

The POET. No, I am not well; I am not happy.   Why
should I be?

ELSA. They are coming, uncle — they are coming!
Why are they coming?

The POET. Coming?   Who?

ELSA. Waldemar and his mother.

The POET. Gertrude Kronborg coming?   I will not
see her.   And you shall not see her son.

ELSA. But, uncle —

The POET. They are not coming!— Put back that book,
I say. (ELSA *replaces the volume.*)   Good. (*To himself.*)
Coming? coming? What possible reason can there be
for that? (*He opens a third journal.*)   Aha! what have
we here?   Three solid paragraphs — half a column, in
short: as I live, a complete biography! "The eminent
dramatic poet. . . . Born at. . . ." Yes, yes; quite cor-
rect. "— in the year . . ." Perfectly, perfectly! "In
his youth traveled extensively in Italy . . . was at Rome
on the memorable occasion of the . . . Supposed to have
drawn thence the inspiration which first moved him to-

ward classic themes . . . the friend of Thorwaldsen . . ."
Admirable! where *did* I lay those scissors? "Old play-
goers will recall his repeated triumphs on the stage of
our own Theater Royal."—But what is this? "The unfortunate series of events which led to his withdrawal from
public view . . . mistaken attitude toward the manage-
ment . . . ill-advised stand against the best critical opinion . . . not altogether mindful of the changes then taking place in the public taste . . ." What, what! Some
enemy has written this! But let me go on calmly. "His
ungallant and inexplicable treatment of that sterling artist
and general favorite, Gertrude Kronborg . . ." No, no;
this is all wrong; it is miserably unjust. It shall have no
place in my album—never! (*He throws down his scissors
and pushes away his paste-pot.*) This is not true. No;
they combined against me; they drove me from the stage;
they ruined my career—those Westergaards, those Grundt-
vigs! And she at the head of them!—she whom I so
loved and trusted, she whom I would so gladly have
made my wife. But let me not think of these things.

One paragraph more Some general reflections and
considerations—all in the past tense: was—had been—
would have been; did — did not — could not. What!
will they bury me before I am dead! There are laurels
here, indeed, but they are tied with crape and spattered
by the mud of slander.

One journal still: will it contain any corrective for all
the injustice of the last? Oh, heavens, what is this? —
"the death, after a painful illness . . . at one time promi-
nent among writers for the stage . . . author of 'Cassan-
dra,' etc. . . . the funeral"—oh, powers above! — "the
funeral, we understand, will take place on the coming Wednesday at Vorstadt, his late residence . . . " Heaven

and earth! they will bury me before I am dead, after all!
Wednesday, Wednesday?—why that is to-day! And Gertrude Kronborg is coming!—she has read these lines, and
she is coming to see me put into my grave!

ELSA (*whose attention is drawn by his signs of surprise
and dismay*). Uncle, uncle, what dreadful thing are you
keeping from me? Why have all these newspapers come,
and what intelligence are you cutting out of them to prevent my learning it? What loss, what death, what misfortune . . . ?

The POET. None, my child, none. You—you spoke
of a manuscript . . .

ELSA. Do you wish to see it now?

The POET. Yes. I must take my thought away from
such . . . You say she is coming?

ELSA. I said he was coming. He may bring her with
him.

The POET. All that must be avoided. Yes, I will look
at it. A woman of fortune and position, I believe you said?

ELSA. Yes; one who has read all your works and long
admired them; one who in her young days wept over
them at the play-house, and who has ever since hoped to
produce something worthy of your approval.

The POET. Let me look at it. Ah—um! "Act Four;
the portico of the temple of Juno,"—a very proper place;
I feel quite at home there. "Lucilius (addressing the Roman cohorts)"—a worthy body of men:—

> Then let the doom of Labicum be sealed!
> Our conquering blades . . . um—um . . .
> . . . . to force a dauntless way
> Till Nelo's helm be cleft . . .

This may well repay examination. One faithful worshipper remains at the true fane.— I will take it to my room. (*To* LISBETH, *who enters.*) You may put this place in order and see that no one disturbs my quiet.— To come to me to-day for advice and approbation — this is the choicest flower of fame! — I may still number myself among the living, I think! (*He goes out.*)

ELSA (*to* LISBETH). Your fate is in his hands. Would that mine (*regarding* WALDEMAR'S *letter*) were in *his!*

[LISBETH quickly brings the disordered room to rights,— desk, bookcase, rug. A knock at the street-door. Enter the LEADING LADY and her SON — both dressed in black.]

LISBETH (*with a deference that approaches solemnity*). Ah, it is Madame Kronborg. And Mr. Waldemar. Be seated, pray. I will let my master know at once that you are here. But he is very busy with an important matter that he has just taken up, and I doubt if he can see you immediately. Seat yourselves, however.

[LISBETH passes out. The new-comers take chairs and look about the room with a mournful interest.]

The LEADING LADY. Busy — I can well believe it: the last sad rites.

WALDEMAR. Who can have charged himself with them? " Her master," she said.

The LEADING LADY. I think there was a brother;— but it is a long time back to those old, old days. Poor Leopold!— it is twenty years since last I saw him.

WALDEMAR. And I have never seen him. But I have felt him.

The LEADING LADY. Hush, Waldemar. You must not say that here.

WALDEMAR. I had lost all hope of ever entering this house. But here I am — because no one along the road could direct us to the proper church.

The LEADING LADY. Poor Leopold! — and there was the day when all the streets were thronged to see him pass! (*They lapse into a decorous and mournful silence.*)

[Another knock at the street-door. Two elderly men, also in black, are admitted by LISBETH. Inasmuch as they advance direct toward the LEADING LADY, LISBETH yields them to her and withdraws. But they speak no word; they shake her hand and then dejectedly seat themselves close to each other on the opposite side of the room.— A long pause.]

The LEADING LADY. It was you, then, who followed behind us. I am so glad that you could come, Kaspar.

The EX-MANAGER. We felt sure that your guidance would bring us to the right place.

The CRITIC. I had no notion where he lived. It must be twenty years since last we saw him. And nearly ten since we have seen one another.

The LEADING LADY. Yes; I retired ten years ago this spring.

The CRITIC. We should all have remained friends.

The EX-MANAGER. He made it difficult.

The LEADING LADY. I am afraid that is true.

The EX-MANAGER. He questioned my judgment. Yet I still think that my hand was firmer on the public pulse than his was.

The CRITIC. And I — I questioned his methods; — truly

to my own regret.   Times were changing; he would not see it.

The LEADING LADY. And he — he questioned my motives.   Yet his success was as dear to me as to himself. Through twenty rehearsals we struggled, with hitches and quarrels and heartburnings; and at last that dreadful day . . .

The EX-MANAGER. We gave him up; we put on another play.   No one was sorrier than I; but nothing else could be done.

The CRITIC. Then he saw a cabal against him.   He refused any concession, rejected every compromise. . . . But it is all over now.

The EX-MANAGER. Yes, it is all over now.— He was a great man in his day.   Are we the only ones to honor him?

The LEADING LADY. Do not ask that.— What do I see lying there on his desk close beside you?   A wreath?

The EX-MANAGER. A wreath, yes.   A wreath of tarnished silver, with a faded ribbon.   The date is here— you should remember it; it was you who placed this wreath upon his brow.

The LEADING LADY. And I shall place it upon his coffin. Can they have waited for my coming to have that done?

[The door opens.   They lapse into a decorous silence. ELSA enters.   WALDEMAR hastens across to her and takes her hand.]

WALDEMAR. My poor, poor Elsa!   This is a sad day for you.

ELSA. Waldemar, you frighten me!   What did your letter mean?   Why are you dressed throughout in black?

5

And who are all these solemn people seated round the room?

WALDEMAR. The lady, Elsa, is my mother. The stout gentleman is Kaspar Westergaard, who was once manager of the Court Theater. The thin one is Grundtvig, the great Grundtvig, who wrote for many years upon the stage. They have come here to honor your uncle.

ELSA. Then let me greet them. I trust he will forgive them.

WALDEMAR. I trust he *has* forgiven them!

ELSA. Do not be so sure. That terrible quarrel!—I know it all by heart; I have lived upon it for years. Still, if he will but see them, but speak to them . . .

WALDEMAR. Child, what do you mean? They have come to honor your uncle's memory — to follow his body to the tomb.

ELSA. To the tomb? To follow him to the tomb? What are you saying? My uncle is not dead!

WALDEMAR. Not dead?

ELSA. By no means. He is alive and well, and in the next room.

WALDEMAR. Alive and well! But we read in the paper that . . . Then, let me tell my mother — she has felt it all so keenly.

ELSA. By all means.— But wait, Waldemar. I see a chance for reconciliation here. Be silent for a while, Waldemar; you have your interests here, too.

[They seat themselves side by side; all five preserve the deepest silence. The POET enters, deep in LISBETH's manuscript.]

The POET (*unconscious of any presence*). Yes, yes, this is distinctly promising; and it is written, too, in a firm, clear

hand.   One may go far when fairly started upon the right
track.   I shall gladly give audience to this extremely clever
and appreciative woman.   A few suggestions, a few cor-
rections . . .

[He starts suddenly at sight of a roomful of strangers.
The three elder ones rise and advance toward him with
faces full of deep commiseration.]

The Leading Lady. Your poor, poor brother!
The Ex-Manager. We heard it, by the merest chance,
only this morning.
The Critic. And have come in all haste; we trust we
are not too late.

[The Poet, coming to himself and to the situation,
bows with an air of shocked solemnity.]

The Leading Lady. I am Gertrude Kronborg.   I created twenty of his heroines.   And this is Kaspar Westergaard —
The Ex-Manager.—who staged twenty of his plays.
And this is Andreas Grundtvig —
The Critic.—who carried their fame as far as his poor
pen would allow.

[The Poet looks from one to another out of the midst
of a maze of conflicting emotions.]

The Leading Lady. We were all old friends of his.
The Ex-Manager. We are come to wipe out an unfor-
tunate past.
The Critic. And to do honor to his worthy memory.

[The Poet bows gravely and turns away his face.]

The Leading Lady. That hapless day!—a thousand times I 've wished its wretched work undone. I knew my lines; I knew them word for word . . .

The Ex-Manager. I set the stage with scenes all new throughout. They went for nothing . . .

The Critic. I should have strained a point, I think, to take the friendliest view . . .

The Leading Lady. I knew my lines, I say. I know them yet:

> Chide not, my sire, nor think my duty fails
> If from this shelt'ring roof I now depart.
> The road divides. I have a father, yes;
> But have I not a lover too . . . ?

The Ex-Manager (*taking up the part of the Roman father*).

> . . . prate not, O girl! My ears are deaf
> To one who 'd scant her filial duty thus.
> No, not for Juno's self . . . Juno's self. . . .

But twenty years have gone; I can recall the words no longer.

The Poet (*breaking in*).

> No, not for Juno's self would I make peace
> Where hate has held this immemorial sway.
> Like all the past, so all the future too!

The Critic. The precise words! I should have used them in my review, I am sure.

The Poet (*proceeding in the person of the Roman lover, while* Waldemar *and* Elsa *look on and listen with a fascinated interest*).

And yet, proud Roman, if perchance thou think'st
To part for aye two loving hearts like ours,
Know we have ways to 'scape thy tyranny
And take good heed lest . . .

Elsa, bring me the *last* volume of the Collected Works.

[He opens the book with quick decision and places it in the Ex-Manager's hand; the three parts are then carried on to the satisfaction of the Critic, the eager interest of Waldemar and Elsa, and the intense delight of Lisbeth, who (poised in the doorway) finds herself fully in her element at last.]

The Poet (*after many cues have been taken and many sounding lines recited*).

And now, stern father, hear my latest word:
Your child and I have made a solemn vow
That naught below the courses of the stars
Shall separate. . . .

The Ex-Manager. Man, who are you? — you, who know his writings word for word — you, whose presence is a living monument to his memory! Why does your voice tremble? Why do your eyes shine with such a light? You might almost be Leopold Heiberg's self!

The Poet. I *am* Leopold Heiberg's self. You have been brought here by a piece of folly all my own, but I am glad you came. The three whom I have so long held in my memory for enemies turn out to be my truest friends — and all the friends I have.

The Leading Lady. Your hand, Leopold!

The Poet. The things that might have been, Gertrude!

The Leading Lady. We will not think of the things that might have been. We will think (Waldemar *and* Elsa *advance*) of the things that are to be.

Waldemar (*as the* Poet *hesitates*). You have spoken for us in your own verses.

The Critic. They are ones I should have cited as very true and just.

The Ex-Manager. Will you refuse your own tribute to your own lines?

The Leading Lady. Come here, Elsa. For a month past I have known of my son's hopes and wished that they might soon be realized.

The Poet. I yield. But that tribute is not the sole one. I hold here a tragedy written by a woman of fortune and position who has asked my judgment . . . Who is this author, Elsa? You have not yet told me her name.

Elsa (*pointing to* Lisbeth *in the doorway*). There she stands.

The Poet. What! Lisbeth! Is this the woman of fortune and position?

Lisbeth (*advancing*). Yes. My position is that of your maid. My fortune is to have served you for twenty years, and I wish no better for twenty more.

The Critic. Bravo! Our Leopold is another Mohammed: he finds his chief disciple in his own household.

Waldemar (*holding* Elsa's *hand*). Mohammed found more than a disciple!

The Ex-Manager. But the play! it shall be read. Whatever its fate, I say this: it has opened for its author a free path to every theater in town.

The Poet (*holding* Gertrude Kronborg's *hand*). More has opened for *me* than that: the way back into the hearts of three good friends.

THE SHIP COMES IN.

THE SHIP COMES IN.

PERSONS.

The LORD OF THE MANOR. A FISHERGIRL, his grand-
His STEWARD.   daughter.
His LIBRARIAN.   An OLD FISHWIFE.
A SERVING-MAID.   A YOUTH, her grandson.
An OLD FISHERMAN.   Other Fisherfolk.

A neglected terrace in front of a dilapidated château.
The château is at the estuary of a river, and its terrace
commands a wide view of a watery land: low-lying shores
help to define an indefinite horizon, and many dim sails flit
by without pausing and without approaching. Level with
the rugged old balustrade rise the masts and chimneys of a
fishing-village, and through the middle of the terrace a
seamed and salt-stained old stairway leads to the beach
below. The time is sunset, and a pinkish glow touches
alike the sky, the sea, and the distant sails. There is a
light breeze.

At one corner of the terrace the LORD OF THE MANOR
lounges on a shabby garden-seat which is set between two
oleanders in tubs of faded green. In attendance upon him
are his STEWARD and his LIBRARIAN.

The LORD OF THE MANOR (*yawning and stretching*). Yes, one day and one night will be enough — as I fore-judged.

The LIBRARIAN. Your stay is short, my lord.

The LORD OF THE MANOR. It will be long enough to serve my purpose.

The STEWARD. We should be glad to hold you here a second day, my lord.

The LORD OF THE MANOR. I leave to-morrow forenoon; I will hear your reports and receive your payments this evening. This monotony wears upon me past all endurance: the same sea; the same sky; the same people — not a single one seeming to have an interest or a hope; even the same girl standing out there on the end of the pier. She has stood there since noon, I think.

The LIBRARIAN. I have noticed her several times. It is Genevieve.

The LORD OF THE MANOR. But wait — *she* may have an interest or a hope. Ah, thank you, Genevieve. For she shades her eyes as she looks out toward the horizon; what is she expecting? And now she seems to be wringing her hands; what has gone amiss?

The STEWARD. She is waiting for the boat. We are all waiting for the boat. The whole town is waiting for the boat.

The LORD OF THE MANOR. Ah! Is it late? I know nothing, you understand, during one of my afternoon naps.

The STEWARD. It usually arrives at midday.

The LORD OF THE MANOR. Daily?

The LIBRARIAN. Daily! Ah, heavens! Fortnightly — no oftener than that.

The LORD OF THE MANOR. Its coming, then, is an event?

The STEWARD. Its coming means everything for m—
for us, for this little community.

The LIBRARIAN. It is our sole connection with the outside world — that world so vast and all unseen.

The LORD OF THE MANOR. Ah, indeed? — There! I
am sure she is wringing her hands once more; — what a
sadly awkward outline she makes! Who is the old man
that goes stumbling out toward her so clumsily?

The LIBRARIAN. He is her grandfather.

The LORD OF THE MANOR. He does not seem to mind
her.

The STEWARD. He has too many cares. It is he, in
effect, who has charge of our village stores. His fore-
thought means meat, drink, light, heat, medicine for all
these hundred souls.

The LIBRARIAN. Yet all his care would go for little
should the boat but fail us.

The LORD OF THE MANOR. I see.— And who is the old
woman crooning to herself at the bottom of my stairway?

The STEWARD. She is the girl's great-aunt; she is Genevieve's great-aunt.

The LORD OF THE MANOR. I remember; I think I saw
her when I was here seven years ago.

The LIBRARIAN. She has been here seventy.

The LORD OF THE MANOR. And what will the boat
bring to *her?* The doctor, perhaps — for she is coughing,
I notice.

The STEWARD. It will bring her the priest and his mass.
To-morrow is one of his Sundays.

The LORD OF THE MANOR. I understand; she is a devotee.— And who is the youth at her side? He has a
bundle between his feet, I judge.

The LIBRARIAN. He is her grandson. He expects to

leave us upon the return of the boat; it is his first venture into the world.

The LORD OF THE MANOR. Much depends, then, upon the boat and its master? Everyone has expectations, it seems,— except myself.

The LIBRARIAN. I have mine, I assure you.

The STEWARD (*to himself*). And I mine. Whose hopes are greater, I wonder — whose needs more pressing?

The LIBRARIAN. The boat must come; it is a matter of the greatest importance to me.

The STEWARD (*to himself*). The boat must come; it is a matter of life and death for me.

The LORD OF THE MANOR. But there are other boats; I see a score upon the horizon now.

The LIBRARIAN. They are always upon the horizon,— as the stars are always in the sky. They never come nearer.

The LORD OF THE MANOR. But we have our own boats here; there are a dozen this moment at my feet.

The STEWARD. They are old and slow and clumsy, and too deep of draught for many of these sandy shallows. Some of them are leaky, and one or two are rotten. They do not go far. This is but a poor little place. You will not forget that, my lord?

The LORD OF THE MANOR. And the next beyond is like it? And the next? And the next still?

The STEWARD. Do not believe them better.

The LORD OF THE MANOR. And from fifty such I draw my living.— Your accounts are prepared? Your payments will be made to-night? . . .

The STEWARD. Your hopes will be moderate, my lord?

The LORD OF THE MANOR. I have not been unindulgent. This evening shall find me just,— neither more nor less.

[A SERVING-MAID advances along the terrace, bearing a tray with refreshment.]

The LORD OF THE MANOR. Ah, this is attentive — very. Whom have I to thank?

The MAID. The housekeeper sends me with it.

The LORD OF THE MANOR. Let me thank her for sending . . . you with it. Or shall I blame her for not sending . . you with it before?

The STEWARD (*with considerable self-consciousness*). Pour, girl. No simpering.

The LORD OF THE MANOR. Nay, let her simper. She simpers very prettily, I 'm sure. Why was n't she allowed to do her simpering before? — Ah, very refreshing, very grateful, I 'm sure — your wine, I mean.

The LIBRARIAN. I am hoping to be able soon to offer your lordship something much more grateful than this.

The LORD OF THE MANOR. Is it possible?

The LIBRARIAN. Might I venture to look for your lordship's acceptance of the dedication of my new work? It is nearing completion.

The LORD OF THE MANOR. What work is this?

The LIBRARIAN. You surely remember; you have been advised of its progress from time to time. I am on the fifth and last volume, and the few books and pamphlets I am looking for to-day will help me to a quick completion Then " The Circumnavigation of the Globe " will be ready for your consideration.

The LORD OF THE MANOR. Ah, the Circumnavigation of the . . . to be sure! This, then, is how you have been spending the last seven years — you have been circumnavigating the globe. And who, in the meantime, has been keeping the worms and the sea-air out of my poor old books?

The LIBRARIAN. They have not suffered.   In all that
time, I — I — I have not once left this place.

The LORD OF THE MANOR. Here, then, is what *you* expect by the boat — more books to rot and to decay.   (*To
the* STEWARD.)   And what do *you* expect?

The STEWARD (*in sudden alarm*). I, sir?   I expect nothing, I assure you.   I have everything that I should have,
everything that — that I could hope to have.

The LORD OF THE MANOR. So much the better — for
you, for me, for everybody.— And this girl who leans sea-
ward over the balustrade? Ninette, Niniche, whatever
they call you . . . What do *you* expect from across the
water?

The MAID (*picking up her tray*). A mere trifle, sir; a
trinket, a remembrancer.   One has been promised me.

The LORD OF THE MANOR. Do you see it coming?

The MAID (*shading her eyes*). I think I do, sir.   I see a
new sail.   It is coming this way.   It is the only one coming this way.   It is our sail; it is our boat, I am sure.

The LIBRARIAN. You are right.   It is coming!   It is
coming!

The STEWARD (*in an undertone of great relief*). At last!
At last!   (*He starts upon a quick descent of the stairway,
but checks himself and returns with an assumption of indifference.*)

The LORD OF THE MANOR. Ah, you expect something,
after all.   What is it?

The STEWARD. You are wrong, quite wrong, indeed.   I
look for nothing — for nothing at all.

[The MAID leans over the balustrade and signals the
appearance of the sail to the FISHERFOLK below.   They
crowd slowly up the stairway for the sake of a wider out-

look. The OLD FISHERMAN and his GRANDDAUGHTER leave the pier and climb upward with the rest.]

The STEWARD. Come, come, good people; you press too closely. Down, down, if you please, to your proper level.

The LORD OF THE MANOR. Do not be too strict; allow them the trifling liberty. This is an event of some importance. It means much to every one — except to me.

The STEWARD. And to me.

The LORD OF THE MANOR. To every one, except to me.

The LIBRARIAN. But what is life to him who has everything and looks forward to nothing?

The LORD OF THE MANOR. Very true.

The OLD FISHERMAN (*upon the topmost step*). It is only a small sail, my lord, and it is only a little boat; but it means everything to us.

The LORD OF THE MANOR. Then may the breeze not fail.

The OLD FISHERMAN. It means bread for our tables, oil for our lighthouse . . .

The OLD FISHWIFE (*coughing*). The comfort of religion for our souls . . .

The FISHERGIRL (*with her head upon the* FISHWIFE'S *shoulder*). Oh, may the priest but come, whatever else be lacking! Let him but bring the priest, whatever else be left behind!

The OLD FISHERMAN. We have waited all day. The twilight is now upon us.

The MAID. Cheer up, cheer up! It is Gilbert's own boat. He will soon be here. Already I feel that necklace round my throat.

[The FISHERGIRL raises her head suddenly, and clumsily makes as if to cross over to the SERVING-MAID.]

The LORD OF THE MANOR. How awkward that girl is — how badly she handles herself! How clumsily she picked her way back along the pier! — I could not but notice.

The STEWARD. Do not ask too much from these peasants. You will find few of them so trim and neat as my niece Ninette.

The OLD FISHERMAN. Yes, that is Gilbert's boat.

The YOUTH. And I am to leave here with him to-night.

The LIBRARIAN. But is he following his usual course?

The OLD FISHERMAN. There is little choice; the breeze is light.

The LIBRARIAN. He is not sailing as I should sail. He has not set his canvas as I should set it.

The OLD FISHERMAN. The boat will touch at the pier within ten minutes.

The LIBRARIAN. He has never come like this before. I cannot believe it is his hand that is at the rudder.

The STEWARD (*taking the* LIBRARIAN *aside*). Is Gilbert an honest man?

The LIBRARIAN. How — honest?

The STEWARD. Is he an honest man?

The LIBRARIAN. You know him as well as I do. He is honest enough — with men: as honest as I am — as honest as you are. With women — that is a different affair.

The STEWARD. With women — that does not matter. Would you trust him with a bag of gold?

The LIBRARIAN. I dare say; I dare say.

The STEWARD. Tell me, tell me! Much depends on that; everything depends on that.

The LIBRARIAN. I have trusted him with my books.

The STEWARD. Ah . . . those books!

The FISHERGIRL (*to the* FISHWIFE, *upon whose shoulder she still hides her face*). Do you see him? Is he at the helm? Is the priest with him?

The FISHWIFE. My eyes are too old for the twilight. I only see that the pink of the sail has turned to gray.

The YOUTH. I see no one — as yet.

The FISHERGIRL. He is in the cabin. The priest is in the cabin too. They are sitting there together.

The OLD FISHERMAN. No; the cabin will be crowded with our stores. We shall have light for our signal; we shall have bacon for to-morrow's dinner.

The LIBRARIAN. He is below. He is searching out my books.

The MAID. Be it above or below, so that he brings me my necklace.

The STEWARD (*to himself*). Be he where he may, so that my gold reaches me within the hour. Or how shall I stop the gap and save myself from ruin?

The FISHERGIRL (*to herself*). He is aboard — it must be so. Another fortnight's waiting would be my death.

[The boat approaches quietly through the dusk, and heads for the beach with little heed to the pier. All — save the LORD OF THE MANOR — swarm down to meet it. — There is a flitting of busy figures through the falling night, and presently a great chorus of discordant cries.]

The LIBRARIAN (*appearing at the top of the stairway*). It is shameful; I am in a rage! That the circumnavigation of the globe should be checked by a single wretched sailor!

The LORD OF THE MANOR. Your books are not aboard?

The LIBRARIAN. Nothing is aboard; nobody is aboard!

6

The LORD OF THE MANOR. But really, now . . . Your thought is too — too self-centered.

The LIBRARIAN. Nothing, I say!   Nothing; nobody!

The MAID (*on a lower step*). My necklace!   Where is my necklace?

The FISHERGIRL (*beside her*). What do you say?

The MAID. My necklace!   He promised to bring me one.

The FISHERGIRL. One from whom?

The MAID. From himself — his own gift.

The FISHERGIRL. His?   Gilbert's?

The MAID. Ay, to be sure.

[The FISHERGIRL staggers blindly down the steps and disappears in the darkness.]

The STEWARD (*climbing up, pale as a ghost*). Nobody aboard!   Nothing aboard!   Nothing absolutely — save a broken oar!   (*To the* SERVING-MAID.)   He and his boat — they have betrayed you, they have betrayed me, they have betrayed everybody!

The LORD OF THE MANOR. What does this mean?   Let lights be brought.

The OLD FISHERMAN (*half-way up the steps*). There is hardly a candle in the place.   The lighthouse itself will be dark to-night.

The OLD FISHWIFE (*beside him*). We have not even candles for a mass.   We have only the stars.

The YOUTH (*flinging aside his bundle*). I am left here still; I shall never get away — I shall never know the world.

[The last of the FISHERFOLK pass slowly down the steps and disperse through the village.]

The LORD OF THE MANOR (*to the* STEWARD). Let lights be brought, I say.

The STEWARD. Lights, my lord? You have heard; — there are none.

The LORD OF THE MANOR. No lights! Am I to go candleless to supper?

The STEWARD. Supper, my lord? You understand; — there is none.

The LORD OF THE MANOR. No supper! Am I to go supperless to bed?

The STEWARD. To bed, my lord?

The LORD OF THE MANOR. Ay, to bed. Do not say there is no bed! Am I to go bedless to . . . ?

The STEWARD (*in deep abasement*). No, my lord. Ninette . . .

The LORD OF THE MANOR. That is not what I meant. I think I meant nothing at all,— I went too far. Send the wretched girl away.

The STEWARD. You may go, Ninette. (*The girl lingers.*)

The LORD OF THE MANOR. And this is your stewardship! The man who professes himself without a care, an interest, an expectation, leaves me to go to bed hungry and in the dark! What more have I to learn, I wonder?

The STEWARD. My lord, there will be a candle or two; not enough to fill a luster, but still enough to eat supper by. You shall have my candle.

The LORD OF THE MANOR. Merci.

The STEWARD. And there will be a supper; not such as you are accustomed to, but enough to go to bed on. You shall have my supper.

The LORD OF THE MANOR. Grand' merci.

The Steward. And there will be a bed; not such as you are entitled to, but . . .

The Lord of the Manor. Tell her to go, I say! Tell the wretched thing to go.

The Steward (*in utter despair*). Go, Ninette. (*The girl leaves.*) Grant me the least indulgence, my lord. Things shall be better to-morrow.

The Lord of the Manor. To-morrow I shall go. Come; bring your books, your papers, your moneys. Redeem yourself by a fair account and a full payment. Come. (*He retires within the château.*)

[Dark, moonless night. After an interval, the sail of the empty boat is raised, and the Steward puts forth alone.]

The Steward (*throwing a pistol, with a splash, into the water*). Second thoughts are best. After all, I have left him something — I have left him a roof over his head!

[As the Steward rounds the end of the pier, a second splash is heard : the Fishergirl has flung herself into the sea.]

AT SAINT JUDAS'S.

AT SAINT JUDAS'S.

. . . . . al fondo che divora
Lucifero con Giuda . . . . .
INFERNO, XXXI.

. . . . . in the abyss which swallows up
Judas with Lucifer . . . . .
LONGFELLOW'S TR.

PERSONS.

The BRIDEGROOM.
The BEST MAN.
The SACRISTAN.

A Procession of priests and
acolytes.
Eight PAINTED WINDOWS.

The sacristy of the church of St. Judas. Time: ten
minutes before noon. A pealing of bells is heard.

The sacristy is a great octagonal room of sculptured
stone; its groined vaulting is upheld by one central column which is wreathed from base to capital with a band
of pale carven flowers, and its eight windows — broad and
high, trefoiled and quatrefoiled — flood both floor and roof
with an endless dapple and ripple of variegated light. Under one of these windows an open door leads into the
church. Through this doorway one sees the chancel
banked with flowers; and above the decorous murmur of
a thousand tongues one hears the tones of the organ and
the voices of the choir-boys.

Present in the sacristy: the BRIDEGROOM and his BEST

MAN. Both are in full uniform; each wears white gloves and carries a sword.

———

The BRIDEGROOM (*gaily*). In ten minutes — ten minutes more!

The BEST MAN (*with constraint*). In ten minutes — as you say.

The BRIDEGROOM (*fastening his glove*). Is that a long time, or a short time? A long time, I think.

The BEST MAN. A short time. But much may happen within a short time; much may happen in ten minutes.

The BRIDEGROOM. How soberly said! Are you as jovial as one's closest friend should be?

The BEST MAN. Perhaps not. This day — it means so much for me.

The BRIDEGROOM (*unfastening his glove*). As much as it means for me?

The BEST MAN. As much, yes. Quite as much. Perhaps more.

The BRIDEGROOM. Not more. For it means everything in the world for me.

The BEST MAN. It means everything in the world for *me.*

The BRIDEGROOM. *Now* that voice vibrates with such a degree of interest as I have felt this day demanded! *Now* I begin to recognize you! — the first time for a month.

The BEST MAN. I am the same. I am unaltered.

The BRIDEGROOM (*refastening his glove*). No, no; you have never been quite the same since I told you — since you heard of the great change in store for me.

The BEST MAN. How did you tell me? In your sleep

— your own pillow close to mine.   I felt myself an eaves-dropper; I felt that I had betrayed your confidence.

The BRIDEGROOM. Not betrayed; only anticipated. You would have known within a day.   You have known everything else.   You have shared my thoughts, my ideas, my secrets, my ambitions.   We have eaten together; we have slept together; we have fought side by side. We are of the same age, the same height — my eyes have always been able to look level into yours.   We are of the same bulk as well; — who shall say that even at the present moment I am not wearing your coat and you mine?

The BEST MAN. That has happened more than once.

The BRIDEGROOM. You have saved my life; I have saved yours.   Have we not pledged an unbreaking friendship?

The BEST MAN. We have.

[The FIRST of the EIGHT WINDOWS comes to life; there is a flux of color and of outline among its mullioned lights. Gradually two figures among its ranks of churchly warriors become strangely secularized; they raise their crossed swords on high, while their left hands meet in a clasp of friendship.   The colors upon the pavement shift in corre-spondence, and from the church, or from spaces far above and beyond it, there come the tones of the *Ecce, quam bonum.*]

The BRIDEGROOM. But for *you* my bones, hacked by African sabers, might now be bleaching upon the desert sands.

The BEST MAN. But for *you* my own, gnawed by name-less fishes, might now be lying at the bottom of the sea.

The BRIDEGROOM. Your arm, sweeping through that burning air, saved me for to-day.

The BEST MAN. Yours, cleaving through those angry waters, saved me for — for — (*to himself*) for — what?

The BRIDEGROOM. Yes, you have saved me for to-day. A moment more, and I shall stand where I have long hoped to stand, and shall take the vow that so long has been ready on my lips. At last all obstacles are brushed aside — at last the way stands clear. Those obstacles — you know my combat with them as well as I myself. At every step, on every hand, this mysterious opposition, this determined and unceasing enmity. From what source could it come? From what motive? What enemy have I? The worst should stay his hand at such a time as this.

The BEST MAN (*vaguely*). True — true.

The BRIDEGROOM. I pass over the attempt to embarrass my fortune; and I will say nothing of the efforts made to transfer me to another regiment and to have me sent back to the wars. Nor will I dwell upon the conspiracy disclosed by the repeated advice from so many friends to forego this marriage. For few of these advisers were close enough to me to have the right to speak; fewer still had any definite reason to tender; and all were but too plainly moved — some of them unconsciously, perhaps — by one hidden yet dexterous hand. Let all that pass. How did the real attack begin? What was the first thing to be insinuated?

The BEST MAN (*as before*). Yes, I remember.

[The SECOND of the EIGHT WINDOWS is endowed with a moving consciousness. Ten honorable Knights rise in a semicircle and look down, with an open apprehension in their pure young eyes, upon the pair beneath. An indig-

nant diapason rolls in from the organ, and distant voices
are heard to chant the *In quo corriget ?*]

The BRIDEGROOM. A shameful whisper, creeping hither
and thither, named me a cheat, a trickster, a gamester. I
have played — yes; it is the privilege of my order, of my
profession. But I have never played otherwise than honorably.

The BEST MAN. Never otherwise than honorably.

The BRIDEGROOM. A hundred tongues came to my defense. Only one was silent — yours. I can never thank
you enough for that. Your perfect confidence would not
deign . . . Your certainty of my innocence made it
seem . . .

The BEST MAN. Unnecessary to defend.

[The Knights look into one another's eyes and shake
their heads and turn away their faces.]

The BRIDEGROOM. I strangled this slanderous report —
though *she* indeed had never doubted me; and I struck
down the only man who dared repeat it openly. But
what came next? After defending my honor as an offi-
cer, I was compelled to defend my honor as a suitor.

[The THIRD WINDOW sets itself in motion. A band of
chaste young Damsels brush forward through ranks of tall
and rigid lilies and curve their lustrous palms before their
ears to hear the coming words of ill-report. Voices (not
theirs) intone the words of the *Noli æmulari.*]

The BRIDEGROOM. A score of lying words placed in an
honest hand — a villainous bit of paper brought to the

gaze of a pair of trusting eyes. Who could have done it, I ask — and why?

The BEST MAN. We never learned.

The BRIDEGROOM. I have indeed lived freely, but who shall say that I have seriously overpassed the bounds?

[The Damsels blush, and stoop to hide their faces among the lilies. But their blushes are repeated upon the pavement.]

The BEST MAN. No one.

The BRIDEGROOM. I went to her brother. What I told him satisfied him. But who could have written that letter? And why?

The BEST MAN. You never learned.

The BRIDEGROOM. But as bad followed — or worse. What was next attacked? My courage as a soldier. Mine — mine!

[The FOURTH WINDOW. An army with banners. The leaders of the host rest on their swordhilts and gaze downward with satirical and contemptuous smiles. Above the ranks rise flags of scarlet and purple that flaunt in airy derision and dapple the sculptured pillar.]

The BRIDEGROOM. I demanded a hearing. I combated the unworthy charges sent back across those wastes of sand and of sea. I summoned my witnesses. *You* spoke for me; briefly, quietly, one might almost have said reluctantly.

The BEST MAN. You were above such accusations.

The BRIDEGROOM. Your words, added to those of others, sufficed. And that evening Angela kissed me for the untarnished soldier that I was.

The BEST MAN. Then I said enough. (*To himself.*)
Too much, perhaps.

[The Leader of the Army lifts a foreshortened sword, and
makes a movement as if of warning. But neither of the
pair interprets his movement, for neither sees it.]

The BRIDEGROOM. I came at last, then, to stand forth
whole, sound, unscathed. I. But the others? — my
bride? her parents? . . .

[The FIFTH WINDOW. A rising of the sheeted Dead.
The sun, half hidden by a passing cloud, but partly pene-
trates the dull and spectral panes.]

The BRIDEGROOM. A rumor ran that my orphaned
bride had been born out of wedlock — that no priest had
ever blessed the union of . . . O, it was foul! I beat at
the doors of town-halls; I rained blows upon the portals of
parish churches: my Angela should not be thus doubly
and disgracefully orphaned. I searched the records, dim
and dusty as they were. And I brought the truth tri-
umphantly to light.

[The sun reappears. The Dead throw back their cowls.
Their eyes sparkle, their cheeks are flushed with life. They
raise their full-fleshed hands in benediction.]

The BRIDEGROOM. But who could have started that
rumor? And why?
The BEST MAN. Who, indeed? You have never
learned.
The BRIDEGROOM. But even that was not enough.

Worse followed — you know what. Word passed that
Angela herself . . . No, no; I cannot say it. I — I
heard that she was false. . . .

[The Sixth Window.   A trio of female figures — Love,
Truth and Purity—entwined in one another's arms.
Their eyes are startled; their garments quiver and scintillate in reds and ambers and pale greens.   Their mouths
open, but whether in condemnation or in defense it is too
soon to say.   From that quarter, or from another, there
comes the chant: *Iniquos odio habui.*]

The Bridegroom.— that she was untrue . . . impure.
. . . Yes, but the last great lie was faced and routed.
Here I await her; one moment more and she will have
come. (*Happy tears course iridescently down the cheeks of
the three Virgins.*)   Hark, hark!   I hear even now their
carriage-wheels without.

[The Sacristan enters.]

The Sacristan. Noon, and past noon.   And the bride
does not come.

The Best Man. The chimes have long since ceased
pealing.

The Sacristan. The whole church questions, and
whispers ; — do you not hear ?

The Bridegroom. Nothing can prevent that.   Let the
bells be heard too.

[The Sacristan closes the door leading into the church,
and retires by means of a second one opposite.   Through
walls, or doors, or windows are heard the words: *Quare
fremuerunt gentes?*]

The BEST MAN. The bells may ring, but they will bring you nothing.

The BRIDEGROOM. What do you mean, my friend?

The BEST MAN. She will not come.

[The SEVENTH WINDOW. The Seven Cardinal Virtues; they change, with a slow but relentless movement of color, of outline, of feature, into the Seven Deadly Sins. This transformation, like all the others, passes unheeded.]

The BEST MAN. She will not come. Have you not heard?

The BRIDEGROOM. Heard what?

The BEST MAN. What every one else has heard; what fills the church with smiles and whispers even now.

The BRIDEGROOM. What have you to tell me?

The BEST MAN. It is always thus. The most concerned is ever the last to learn.

The BRIDEGROOM. What have I to learn?

The BEST MAN. This: that she has sinned.

The BRIDEGROOM. That should have been said before. Or, better and more truly, not at all.

The BEST MAN. They say that she has sinned, and sinned — with me.

The BRIDEGROOM. O, my enemy! unseen, but unrelenting! And what is your response?

The BEST MAN. Were the other reports true?

The BRIDEGROOM. Not one of them.

The BEST MAN. Ah . . . Perhaps the chimes will begin again. Perhaps the bride will yet appear. Perhaps those whisperings will cease. Do you hear them?

The BRIDEGROOM. Yes — even through that door.

The BEST MAN. Do you hear the bells?

The BRIDEGROOM. No.

The BEST MAN. Do you hear the bride arriving?

The BRIDEGROOM. Not yet.

The BEST MAN. Ah . . .   [A pause.

The BRIDEGROOM. Is it true — what you say? Is it true? Is it true?

The BEST MAN. Why need that matter? It is nothing; let it pass.

The BRIDEGROOM. Nothing? . . . Let it pass? . . .

The BEST MAN. Yes. *I* am here. And *she* will never be. You may wait, but you shall wait in vain. (*He places his hand upon the other's shoulder.*) If she were to come, I should not let her have you. She shall not have you. Nobody shall have you.

The BRIDEGROOM. What is your meaning, Oliver?

[The Deadliest of the Seven Sins hides her face; it is too hideous for contemplation.]

The BEST MAN. I shall not let you go. Our friendship has been too long, too close, too intimate. It shall not be destroyed; it shall not be broken. No one shall come between us.

The BRIDEGROOM. Peace, Oliver, in heaven's name!

The BEST MAN. Why have we lived so long together — why shared each other's every thought? To be completely sundered now? — Why did I save your life? To have it taken from me thus? — Why did you save mine? That you might cast this blight upon it in the end? — She shall not have you! I will do everything to prevent it! I *have* done everything to pre— . . .

The BRIDEGROOM. Ha! It is *you* who have attacked my honor?

The BEST MAN. Your honor is secure.

The BRIDEGROOM. It is *you* who have questioned my courage?

The BEST MAN. You are brave; I believe that.

The BRIDEGROOM. It is *you* who have insulted my love?

The BEST MAN. No one loves you more than I.

[The sculptured wreath entwined round the great central column writhes in descending spirals, like a vast serpent.]

The BRIDEGROOM. You are a liar, a traitor, a perjurer, and you shall die.

The BEST MAN. One of us shall die.

The BRIDEGROOM. One of us two shall die. It shall be you.

The BEST MAN. One of us shall die — one of us three. *She* shall die; it is she who has come between us.

The BRIDEGROOM (*drawing his sword*). You shall die. I shall kill you with my own hands.

[The chimes begin to ring. A sound of rumbling wheels and trampling hoofs is heard outside. A procession of priests and acolytes crosses the sacristy on the way into the church. They pause at the signs of combat.]

The BRIDEGROOM. Ah! She comes! She believes in me! And so shall all the others! They do, already; I will not believe the throng makes sport of our fair fame. (*To the priests.*) Move on; move on! I will follow you within a moment.

[The procession traverses the sacristy and moves on toward the high altar. The BRIDEGROOM shuts the door be-

7

hind it. The BEST MAN, springing forward, thrusts him
from it, and then stands staunchly with his own back
against its panels.]

The BEST MAN. You shall not pass. You shall never
pass—to her.

The BRIDEGROOM. Stand aside. Let me through.

The BEST MAN. I do not mean to fail at the last moment. I shall not allow so many good endeavors to go
for naught.

The BRIDEGROOM. Stand aside. I hate you; I detest
you; I despise you; I loathe you.

The BEST MAN. You hate me? That cannot be!

The BRIDEGROOM. I hate you with my whole heart. I
loathe you with my whole soul.

The BEST MAN. You loathe me? I, who have done
so much . . .

The BRIDEGROOM. You are not fit to live. You are
not fit to die. But die you shall. I shall not kill you.
You shall kill yourself. You shall do it now, and I shall
see you do it. You have no other road to redemption.

The BEST MAN. We have been friends always . . . I
have loved you all my life . . . The thought of *her* made
me mad—made me desperate . . .

The BRIDEGROOM. Time presses. Use your blade.

[The EIGHTH WINDOW. The Angelic Host trumpeting
from the clouds, while Lucifer plunges headlong toward
the Pit: the wonder is that he can fall so long, so fast, so
far.

When the BRIDEGROOM opens the door into the church,
the BRIDE is seen coming up the aisle, while the choir-
boys and the organ unite in a resounding Gloria. Upon

the floor of the sacristy lies the body of a man in a pool of blood.   As the BRIDE and the BRIDEGROOM meet before the altar rail, the EIGHT WINDOWS, dappling the floor of the sacristy with a thousand varied splotches of color — (but there is one, broader and brighter than them all) — shudder back convulsively to their pristine selves.]

THE LIGHT THAT ALWAYS IS.

THE LIGHT THAT ALWAYS IS.

PERSONS.

The JOURNEYMAN.
The DEVOTEE.
The OLD CAMPAIGNER.
The HOUSEHOLDER.

Various members of his
Family.
TWO PROCESSIONS, and an
ARMY on the march.

The porch of the almshouse of St. Just. Palings and clipped box-trees screen it from the highroad that runs through the village; and the thatched cottage of the HOUSEHOLDER, over the way, is its nearest neighbor.

———

The DEVOTEE (*folding his withered old hands*). No, I have never married.

The OLD CAMPAIGNER (*smoothing an empty sleeve*). Nor I.

The DEVOTEE. The church itself has been the sheltering roof above my head; the glow of the high altar has kept me warmer than any hearth-fire could have done; and in the companionship of the great body of true believers have I found the comforts and consolations of the home circle. I have saved my own soul; I have never dared—nor wished—to impose the same hard task upon another soul.

The CAMPAIGNER. I do not claim to have saved my soul, but up to this time I have saved my body — no lighter thing, believe me. Nor shall I claim to have withheld your hard task from another; but I have never married — if that is what you mean. My sword was my bride; my general was my divinity. Between them, they kept me busy, interested, satisfied.

The HOUSEHOLDER. And can either of you believe that he has done his full duty toward himself and toward the world? Both of you have lost the real joy and significance of life . . .

The DEVOTEE. I have found the duty of life to lie in a praise of the divine goodness and a heed to the divine decrees.

The CAMPAIGNER. And I have found the chief joy and significance of life to lie in the impressing, so far as might be, of my own will and power on other men.

The DEVOTEE. I have never lagged behind my leader.

The CAMPAIGNER. Nor I, believe me, behind mine.

The HOUSEHOLDER. But neither of them has led you by the true path to the true goal; neither has led you, through the joys of a first love, to your own roof-tree, to your own hearth-stone, to the loving ministrations of a wife, to the affectionate caresses of a flock of happy children.

The DEVOTEE. You may be right; but my duty —

The HOUSEHOLDER. *Your* duty? *My* duty — everybody's duty; his duty toward himself, toward woman, toward society, toward the divine intention.

The DEVOTEE. Have you taken all your crosses upon yourself — ?

The HOUSEHOLDER. You shall not call them crosses!

The DEVOTEE. — all your crosses upon yourself from a sense of duty? I will maintain that you had no thought of duty; you followed merely your inclinations. You were prompted by simple selfishness and self-indulgence.

The HOUSEHOLDER. I, the father and protector of a half-score of children, to be accused of selfishness, of self-indulgence! Through all these cruel times of war and want, bread has never yet failed beneath my roof.

The CAMPAIGNER. Can you believe that you actually entered upon the thorny path of matrimony — ?

The HOUSEHOLDER. You shall not call it a thorny path!

The CAMPAIGNER.— upon the thorny path of matrimony from a pure sense of duty? No; you were impelled by necessity— the necessities of your own nature. Passion started you, and the momentum of mere habit has carried you along.

The HOUSEHOLDER. These words to me, the head and mainstay of the village! Through all this year of violence and of outrage no harm has come to a single soul within our bounds.

The DEVOTEE. Do not hint at our helplessness.

The CAMPAIGNER. Do not taunt us with our poverty.

The DEVOTEE. My prop has never failed me; my reward will come in good season.

The CAMPAIGNER. Mine has come already. I am indeed old and broken and crippled, but my country gives me my daily pipe and glass, and my window, opening upon the highway, shows me all the world as it passes by.

The DEVOTEE. I am equally well housed here, and equally content. I think of answered prayers, of prosperity for the just, of the coming unity of man beneath the sheltering wings of a universal mother-church. I have but one wish: breath and ardor to add my prayers to those of all the good men who cry for the passing of our present evils—this cruel and lingering war, this scarcity throughout the land, this sickness and suspense within our houses.

The CAMPAIGNER. And I but one regret: that I can no longer mount my charger and draw my saber and help to hunt these villainous intruders from our land. Our men may march by before many hours are spent; yet I can do no more than stand within this porch and wave a single arm at their victorious passing. But there have been other and different days: days of smoke and flame, days of thundering charges, days of triumphal entries; and that day when the Commander himself fastened this medal upon my breast.

The HOUSEHOLDER. To such a wish and to such a regret, I add one firm intention: to hold my own, to cherish and protect my family, and to remain the firm, true head of this little community.

[The JOURNEYMAN, with his tools slung across his shoulder, comes singing along the highway.]

The HOUSEHOLDER. Here comes a careless fellow. Little matters it to him that we are in the midst of war and of scarcity, or that almost every household has its sick wife or its ailing child . . .

The CAMPAIGNER. But his song is not a merry one.

The JOURNEYMAN (*coming up*).   Is it a sad one?

The HOUSEHOLDER. No. But why do you sing at all? — for lack of thought?

The JOURNEYMAN. For rest from thought.

The DEVOTEE. Have you to think at your work?

The JOURNEYMAN. Not at all. The movement of my hand alone is enough to engage and satisfy me.

The HOUSEHOLDER. You will not think between times on the road? You wish never to think at all?

The JOURNEYMAN. You have it. Thought is a sad mistake. Avoid it as far as possible.

The HOUSEHOLDER. That may do for one who would seem to have no home, no family, no responsibilities, no cares.

The JOURNEYMAN. You are right. I have no ties, no settled habitation. I simply fling my tools across my back and trudge along the road from place to place. I am current everywhere. I see everything that goes on — do you wonder that I hardly care to think?

The HOUSEHOLDER. But *I* think — I must; — for my home, my family. Ah, young man, you lose the crowning joy of life. To be the ruler of your own fireside, the center of a circle of loving and ministering—

[Angry voices come across from the HOUSEHOLDER's dooryard. A middle-aged woman and a grown girl are seen in violent altercation. A number of young boys, a second brood apparently, tug with inimical intent at the girl's ankles and elbows.]

The CAMPAIGNER. Cross over in the interests of peace!
[The HOUSEHOLDER leaves.]

The DEVOTEE. The stepdaughter does not take kindly to the new rule.

The JOURNEYMAN. Our friend has been married once before, then?

The CAMPAIGNER. Twice. His first wife died in childbed, leaving a numerous flock behind her. I have heard her spoken of as an idle and wasteful creature.

The DEVOTEE. His second drove all the elder of her stepchildren from home, and her cruelty or her neglect

soon reduced the number of the younger.   Then she herself left—with another woman's husband.

The JOURNEYMAN. And the third?

The CAMPAIGNER. You have seen her—and heard her.
The sick child now beneath that roof must be charged to
her indifference.

The JOURNEYMAN. And that quarrel—what was its
nature?

The CAMPAIGNER. It was religious.

The DEVOTEE. No; it was merely domestic.

The CAMPAIGNER. It was the clash of rival faiths.

The DEVOTEE. Not at all; it was simply the clash of
contending authorities.

The JOURNEYMAN. I should have supposed his home
life one of great peace and felicity.   Yet he seemed to reproach me for my single state—for my having failed to
add to the sum total of the human race, and by conse-
quence to the sum total of human happiness.   I take some
credit, however, for never having forced an earthly career
upon a single human soul: no struggle, no suffering, no
injustice, no poverty, no temptation, no damnation, no
fight through the thorny paths of a world where only one
out of a hundred is the right one.

The DEVOTEE. I agree with you most heartily.   But—

The CAMPAIGNER. And I.   Yet—

The DEVOTEE. I myself have never sought happiness in
married life.   However—

The CAMPAIGNER. And I—I never could have found
it there.   Nevertheless—

The JOURNEYMAN. But, yet, however, nevertheless . . . ?

The DEVOTEE. Yet matrimony is an approved and ac-
cepted arrangement.

The CAMPAIGNER. And we are bound to acknowledge

that it has brought safety to many souls and happiness to many hearts.

The DEVOTEE. I could not attempt to save others; I have found it hard enough to save myself. I should not care for the responsibility of new souls; but if prayers, fasts, scourgings can placate the powers above—if submission to the divine will can ransom my own soul . . .

The JOURNEYMAN. You think, then, to have fathomed the intentions of the ruling power?

The DEVOTEE. Yes.

The JOURNEYMAN. And to have found the way to placate and to please the unseen orderer of all?

The DEVOTEE. Yes.

The JOURNEYMAN. Then you have done the great thing. I should reverence you—if you stood alone in this. But others have done the same. I should reverence them, too, if the conclusion of each were not at variance with the conclusion of every other—and probably with yours, as well.

The DEVOTEE. There is but one true belief; there is but one true way.

The JOURNEYMAN. Yours, doubtless.—But you spoke of prayer. Can you pray?

The DEVOTEE. I can. I do—daily—hourly. I do little else.

The JOURNEYMAN. Then fall to your work. For an enemy is marching down upon you. Meet it betimes.

The DEVOTEE. We have met it already; we are preparing to meet it again to-day. If prayers, processions, banners, observances, supplications can aught avail . . .

The CAMPAIGNER. Truly, our scarcity is not yet a famine.

The DEVOTEE. Nor can our sickness yet be termed a

plague. And what has stayed the advance of starvation
and of—

The JOURNEYMAN. Again I say it—an enemy is marching toward you.

The DEVOTEE. I know your meaning; but do not remind
me of the importunities of that band of hateful heretics.—
What, I ask you again, has stayed the advance of starvation and of pestilence if not the supplications of pure and
trusting hearts?—Hark! here is your answer.

[A kind of wailing chant is heard a little distance down
the roadway. It is immediately echoed, with a difference,
from the opposite direction, and two processions of suppliants advance and meet in the highway before the almshouse. The leader of one procession wears a broad cloak
of embroidered yellow silk; the leader of the other wears
a long, close black coat. The one procession depends
chiefly upon a big purple banner; the other upon a multi-
tude of little black books. The one is joined by the
HOUSEHOLDER and his daughter; the other by the HOUSE-
HOLDER'S wife.]

The CAMPAIGNER. I *said* it was a religious quarrel.

The JOURNEYMAN. Is this the time for any quarrel at
all?

The DEVOTEE (*viewing one of the processions with an
angry disgust*). Is that the way to walk? Is that the way
to turn one's eyes? Is that the way to fold one's hands?
Is that the tongue for addressing the throne of grace? No
wonder that plenty is not restored! No wonder that pestilence is but barely withheld! No wonder that our own
people are preparing to dispute their passage!—(*He looks
about anxiously.*) Where is it? Where did I lay it?

The JOURNEYMAN. What?

The DEVOTEE. My stick.

The JOURNEYMAN. You would not beat them?

The DEVOTEE. They shall not nullify our prayers! They shall not weary the heavenly patience! There!— the first blow is struck! Let me hasten to the support of the true cause.

[The people of the two processions have attacked one another with staves. Villagers flock out of the neighboring cottages, and many brethren issue from the almshouse itself, while others, in various stages of disability, look out through its windows. All immediately take sides, as prompted by prejudice, association, early education. The DEVOTEE enters into the struggle with a hearty good will, while the CAMPAIGNER, beating upon his bench with his crutch, encourages both sides with his shrill crow. The HOUSEHOLDER is belabored by his own wife, whose clothing, in turn, is torn by her enraged stepdaughter.]

The DEVOTEE (*shouting back to his associates from the edge of the press*). Victory! victory!

The JOURNEYMAN. I see no victory. How does he mean?

The DEVOTEE (*coming nearer*). Look! our banner holds the roadway, and our people are forming a solid mass all round it!

The CAMPAIGNER. And the others are forming another on the green for a second attack upon it.

The DEVOTEE (*sinking upon his knees and beginning a voluble prayer in the dust of the roadway*). Let it be a lasting triumph for the true Faith —

The CAMPAIGNER. And the one Hope —

The JOURNEYMAN. And the only real Charity!

The DEVOTEE (*rising, after many phrases of passionate pleading*). I shall be heard — and answered.

The JOURNEYMAN. Perhaps. But I have known the just to pine on prayer while the evil were fattening on blasphemy. I have known all response to be withheld when truth, justice, every good instinct of the heart called for heed, for grace, for an interposing miracle indeed. So I have taken a middle course — and silence has neither thinned me nor fattened me. Even were I to pray, but one thing would make me more ashamed than to call down curses upon an enemy.

The HOUSEHOLDER (*coming back with a bleeding face*). What is that?

The JOURNEYMAN. To clamor incessantly that benefit and profit might descend upon myself.

The CAMPAIGNER. I agree with what you say. Yet —

The HOUSEHOLDER. And I. Still —

The CAMPAIGNER. True, one should not be too unforgiving toward one's neighbor. All the same —

The HOUSEHOLDER. Nor too importunate for one's self. Notwithstanding —

The JOURNEYMAN. Yet, still, all the same, notwithstanding . . . ? Continue.

The CAMPAIGNER. Still, we are poor creatures dependent upon a higher power. It may fail us sometimes, but not always.

The HOUSEHOLDER. And there is comfort in the thought that our poor little affairs may be found to have the importance at a distance that they seem to have here close at hand.

The DEVOTEE. There is no distance. All evils are as near to Heaven as to us.

The JOURNEYMAN. Then pray, pray, pray! Fall to it — all three of you. Pray for yourselves — and for Heaven too. For a great evil is drawing near.

The HOUSEHOLDER. What evil?

The JOURNEYMAN. I have told you already: an army. They are behind me. Listen; do you not hear the sound of bugle-notes and the distant tramp of many hoofs?

The CAMPAIGNER. An army? Then it is our own; no other is near.

The DEVOTEE. Our own? Then you shall see them march past in triumph. Else why have I prayed night and morning in the parish church for their success?

The CAMPAIGNER. They are coming! they are coming! Many a long day have I hoped to see them pass.

The HOUSEHOLDER. I even see the leaders and the dust of their advance. But what have we to fear? They are our own men.

The JOURNEYMAN. An army is an army.

The CAMPAIGNER. Receive them with open arms. Give them of your best . . .

[The fight in the roadway is resumed. The HOUSE-HOLDER and the DEVOTEE, with no further heed to the advancing host, reënter the struggle. The HOUSEHOLDER is beaten by his wife's brother, and jeered by his own children.]

The JOURNEYMAN. Your advice is good; these villagers will do well to heed it. Let them give their best — all the more so, that their best is but indifferent. An army is an army — none the less so, an army in retreat.

The CAMPAIGNER. An army in retreat? But you said it was *our* army.

8

The JOURNEYMAN. It *is* our army. Can both sides win?

The CAMPAIGNER. In my time our side always did. Could you but have seen our hussars in action you would have felt the reason why. In our blue and gold we swept the field as a scythe shears a meadow — as bright, as keen, as quick, as resistless. Nothing withstood us. We cut down horse and man alike, just as the —

The JOURNEYMAN. Why?

The CAMPAIGNER. Why? Because our leader's saber beckoned us onward.

The JOURNEYMAN. What led your leader?

The CAMPAIGNER. What led him?

The JOURNEYMAN. Yes,— what was the cause?

The CAMPAIGNER (*hesitating*). The cause was our country's, I suppose. Yes, it was for our country that we fought.

The JOURNEYMAN. Perhaps. Men have fancied themselves fighting for their country when they were only fighting for a sect, a dynasty, a despot; for some foul and selfish cause too cleverly disguised for recognition; for mere love of fighting's sake,— from an excess of animal passion or of animal spirits.

The CAMPAIGNER. You shall not question the motives of our soldiers,— any more than you shall question their bravery, their skill, their patient self-denial and endurance —

The JOURNEYMAN. No one will question their patience and endurance — as they file past.

The CAMPAIGNER (*in response to approaching sounds*). They are coming indeed. But you shall not call it a retreat. It is a change of base; it is a piece of strategy to lure the enemy to destruction.

The JOURNEYMAN. Phrase it as you please. But mere words will put neither sound shoes on their feet, nor strength into their tired limbs, nor food into their flapping stomachs.   See for yourself.

[The struggle of the village zealots is brought to an end by the passage of the first division of the Army.   Many hundreds on foot, splashed with mud, stiffened with sweat, swathed in bandages, famished with hunger.   Others limp alongside an extended ambulance-train, and others still, in various stages of dilapidation and disability, straggle here and there over the borders of the wide roadway.]

The CAMPAIGNER (*with reproach, to the returning* DE-VOTEE).   This, then, is your victory ?   I could have prayed a better one myself!

The DEVOTEE. You need not taunt me.   It is not for you to say how a petition is to be answered, or when.   A lesser favor may be withheld that a greater one may be vouchsafed.   Wait for the end.

[The passage of an artillery-train.   Hungry and ex-hausted horses stumble along, dragging miry and disabled gun-carriages.   The men astride throw famished scowls in the direction of storehouses and barnyards.]

The CAMPAIGNER. Poor fellows!   But they need not stare at our orchards; those were stripped long ago.

The DEVOTEE. Nor need they peer at our hen-houses; every perch has been vacant for a month.

The CAMPAIGNER. Their eyes are sharp.   They can see through stone walls.   I should advise no one to bolt doors or to put up bars.

[Other regiments of infantry, embarrassed by a great number of sick, disabled and wounded.   A group of officers who pick their way along mechanically, with lax bridles and downcast eyes. The HOUSEHOLDER and his wife are seen in another altercation upon their doorstep.]

The JOURNEYMAN. She would close the door. Her husband will do well to persuade her to a seeming hospitality.

The CAMPAIGNER. They need it; they deserve it.— But oh, this is not what my memory has pictured through all these years as war!

[The foot-soldiers, attracted by the defensive posture of the HOUSEHOLDER's wife, begin to scale the wall and to trample up through the garden toward the doorstep. Others of their number give a like attention to neighboring houses, which the people of the two broken processions run to protect; a few heads even look over the almshouse palings.]

The CAMPAIGNER. He must let them have their way with the granary and the bakehouse.

The DEVOTEE. May he but keep them from the bedchamber of his sick child!

The CAMPAIGNER. And from the nooks and crannies of his chimney-place!

The JOURNEYMAN. He is a rich man?

The DEVOTEE. He has put something by.

[A squadron of cavalry moves past slowly. Among them is the HOUSEHOLDER's eldest son.]

The CAMPAIGNER. My old regiment! The old flags, the old uniforms of blue and gold, even one or two of the old officers! To think of our parades and sallies and charges! To recall our assaults and sacks, our medals and our triumphal entries! Let me dwell on our address, our courage, our daring, our glory—!

[Several of the horsemen dismount, and join the foot-soldiers in their raid on cottage and barnyard. The HOUSEHOLDER'S son leads the way.]

The CAMPAIGNER. And if that glory now seems the least shade dimmed, it will yet shine forth—and soon, believe me.

The JOURNEYMAN. Glory? I see none. I see only—

The DEVOTEE. Look! how he forces his way in! He has never forgiven his father.

The CAMPAIGNER. And he has never forgotten the nooks and crannies!

The JOURNEYMAN. Let us hope that he will not forget his sick sister—in his career of glory. Glory? I see none. I see only the enlistment of brute force and brute passion in a cause which is but too often only half-understood, and a love of display, indulgence and adventure at the expense of justice, industry and happiness. I have never killed a fellow-creature alone and in my working-clothes; and I hope never to have to do so in company and in uniform.

The HOUSEHOLDER (*hastening across*). Well said. Hope, too, that you may never help to devastate the homes of an honest country-folk like a flock of devouring locusts, that you may never chase their pigs and lambs through the byways saber in hand, and that your friends and neighbors may not stand in idle talk while the work of destruction is going on! Come back and help me!

The DEVOTEE. We could be of no use to you. And see; the last of them are leaving your precincts now.

The CAMPAIGNER. Have they left you your gold?

The HOUSEHOLDER. My gold? There was none. The last went yesterday. But they are meaning to leave a hundred of their sick and dying upon our outskirts.

The JOURNEYMAN. They will do that?

The HOUSEHOLDER. All that, and more. They are indeed moving on; but they have turned our scarcity into famine and our sickness into pestilence.

The CAMPAIGNER. Do not revile them. They must live. They fight for us.

The JOURNEYMAN. They themselves do not know why they fight. A curse upon their leader and upon his selfish ambitions!

The HOUSEHOLDER. And so say I. But—

The DEVOTEE. I too. Still—

The HOUSEHOLDER. Indeed, they should not rob us of our sustenance. However—

The DEVOTEE. Nor should they fan the flames of hatred and animosity. Yet, despite all that—

The JOURNEYMAN. But, still, however, despite all that...? Conclude.

The HOUSEHOLDER. Still, the defense of one's life and country and interests is indeed a glorious and ennobling work.

The DEVOTEE. And the devotion, the discipline, the self-abnegation demanded by the army is hardly less than that exacted by the church itself.

The CAMPAIGNER. Ay, now you speak as one might look to hear you speak!

The HOUSEHOLDER. True, they have swept us clean and drained us dry, but they have still left us the best things of all: the family roof-tree, the cheery hearthstone, the tender care and sympathy of wife and children.

The DEVOTEE. True, they have thoughtlessly trampled our sacred banner underfoot, and have despitefully entreated the little flock of the faithful; but our hope (and theirs, as well) still survives and flourishes — we know none the less surely the divine will and the divinely ordered way to salvation.

The CAMPAIGNER. True, they have just passed us wearied and famished and footsore, but they have remained victor of many a well-contested field in the past, and they will rise to greater heights of glory and of triumph in the future.

[A long pause, during which the JOURNEYMAN bestows upon the other three a close and studious regard.]

The JOURNEYMAN. You puzzle me; you dumfound me. You have shown me man in his three most important relations — his relation to woman, to his fellow-man and to his maker; his relations in War, in Religion and in Domesticity. And in each case I have found you most fantastically illogical. You (*to the* HOUSEHOLDER) chant of the joys of the domestic hearth and of the blessedness of the home circle; yet your wife is a shrew, your children are undutiful, your house is a buzzing and stinging hive of hates and rivalries —

The HOUSEHOLDER (*indignant*). And what of that? Would you have me forget those early days of courtship, my marriage, the birth of my first baby, the little family that grew and gathered round the old hearthstone? Will you deny man the hope, through all his disappointments, that his deepest longings may yet some day be gratified? Go; I cannot see things as you seem to see them.

The JOURNEYMAN. Ah!—And you (*to the* OLD CAM-PAIGNER) you prate of the glory of arms and of the joys of battle. But you have met with injustice full-armed and with cruelty triumphant; and you have just seen your invincibles drag past, torn, muddy, bleeding, despondent, defeated; and you find yourself stranded here, after years of service, subsisting on a mere pittance doled out grudgingly by an indifferent country.

The CAMPAIGNER (*enraged*). And what of that? Would you have me forget my first uniform, my maiden sword, the earliest deed of bravery for which I was promoted and decorated? Would you weaken the allegiance that has been my lifelong stay? Would you withdraw from me the belief, held through all my hardships, that there can be no failure of reward for a lifetime of faithful and willing service? Go; I do not see things as you seem to see them.

The JOURNEYMAN. Aha!—And you (*to the* DEVOTEE) you must have the memory of many unanswered prayers, of many vain cries for Heaven's justice, of many other shameful sectarian struggles than to-day's alone; and not only you, but others too, must sometimes feel the futility of attempting to interpret the divine intentions and of assuming to guard the sole path that leads to salvation.

The DEVOTEE (*with a shrill anger*). And what of that? Would you ask me to forget my dawning aspirations toward the pure and the eternal, my first communion, my earliest years spent among a holy and learned brotherhood? Would you tear down the only prop that sustains me, and deny me another world whose pleasures shall make up for the pains of this? Go; I do not wish to see things as you see them.

The JOURNEYMAN. You amaze me; you sadden me — so far are you astray on every point that vitally concerns the human race!

The HOUSEHOLDER. Who are you, man, that would rob us of all that makes earth dear and life worth living?

The CAMPAIGNER. I half know; I have heard of the passing of such a one through the world.

The DEVOTEE. I know beyond all doubt: he is *the man who sees things as they are.*

[They rise, expressing varying degrees of dread, anger and repugnance, and make as if to retire within the door-way.]

All THREE. Leave us! Go your way!

The JOURNEYMAN (*picking up his tools preparatory to departure*). I do so. I leave you in the fool's paradise created by yourselves and illumined by the light that such eyes as yours require: the light that is, that always has been, that (perhaps) always will and must be. Never leave those precincts; you will be happier there than you ever could be anywhere else. But you have given me cause for thought — you will keep me unhappy for the rest of the day. Yet I have my remedy — work. For I am man in his fourth relation — his relation to his own subsistence, to his own continued existence in the world. I shall resume my toil at once — to-morrow shall find me too busy for thought, too busy for unhappiness.— Farewell.

[He goes.]

THE DEAD-AND-ALIVE.

THE DEAD-AND-ALIVE.

PERSONS.

The NEW LITTLE NUN.   Her LOVER.
                Many Dead Nuns; among them:
An AGED NUN.   A NUN of FORTY.
An ELDERLY NUN.   A YOUNG NUN.
                Several living Nuns; among them:
The ABBESS.

Midnight in the cloister of the Convent of the *Sepolte-Vive* — the Buried-Alive: a Romanesque quadrangle which is flooded with moonlight and planted thick with flat tomb-stones.   Above one side of this enclosure rise the gable of the chapel and the loggia of the belfry.   On the opposite side one divines the roofs of a sleeping city and half hears the murmur of the sea a hundred feet below.   In the dis-tance a mountain-peak burns and glows as if tipped with an enormous live coal and sends a thin veil of smoke down its own dark sides to wander far and wide along a sinuous shore.

———

The NEW NUN (*half hidden in the arched and pillared shade*).   Have I done well? — Whom have I, save myself, to voice an answer?

[The organ-notes from the chapel cease. The light in the window under the gable vanishes. The Nuns, with the Abbess at their head, issue from the chapel, cross the enclosure, and disperse among their cells. From the belfry there comes the stroke of twelve.]

The NEW NUN. Alone with the green moonlight and the gray tombstones. Cut off from the world completely and forever. For me, henceforth, there *is* no world. Never again shall I see the sky, save the small segment overhead. Never again shall I tread the grass, save such as may grow between these marble slabs. Never again shall I see the face of father, mother, sister, friend; never again hear one word that may tell me of their fate or their fortune; and never will one of them, even through a tolling bell, learn aught of mine. They and their world no longer exist for me; I and my world (if world it may be called) no longer exist for them.

[The air begins to become strangely close and oppressive. The bats flit uneasily beneath the shadowed vaulting of the arcades.]

The NEW NUN. And what of Angelo? Nothing. For me he lives no longer; he is dead, like the others. He never should have lived; he never deserved to live. False — faithless; yet I believed in him. I believed against belief, against reason, despite a hundred warnings. He went — and he did not return. Let him remain away; his return would be nothing now.

[A distant sound, as if of iron at work on stone : a sound that is cautious, yet determined, energetic, even desperate.

At the same time the tombstones grate uneasily upon their foundations.]

The NEW NUN. Our wedding-day was set. He did not come. I hoped till hope was useless; I waited, and waiting went for naught. Then I came here. I could think of no better place.

[The distant sound seems nearer; it rings with a passionate and high-hearted energy. At the same time the gravestones shift and heave, as if about to lift and to disclose their secrets.]

The NEW NUN. What shall I find here?—I am too new to know. Peace, let me hope; refuge too, I beg, from the cruelty of human eyes.

[The sound draws nearer still; it seems close to the dusky corner into which the NEW NUN has shrunk.]

The NEW NUN. What do I hear? What sound so strange and yet so near at hand?

[The tombstones jar and labor, and the DEAD NUNS, clad in conventual garb, rise from their graves. They congregate in the middle of the cloister.]

A YOUNG NUN. Why are we summoned?
A NUN OF FORTY. How, rather, are we summoned?
An ELDERLY NUN. But one thing could accomplish this: the presence of a lover.
The YOUNG NUN. How do you know that?
The ELDERLY NUN. I have seen it happen once before—almost.

The NUN of FORTY. Almost?

The ELDERLY NUN. It was in my young days. I was a midnight watcher. I heard sounds such as we hear now —listen! I saw these gravestones heave and sway. I ran to the Abbess. A young man was found working his will upon our walls. He was taken—in time. The stones resumed a quiet that has never been broken till now.

The YOUNG NUN. What became of the man?

The ELDERLY NUN. You are not to ask. None ever learned his fate; it was in the old days . . .

The NUN of FORTY. You told, you say. Should we go and tell now?

An AGED NUN. Tell? tell? Do you think we could?

The NUN of FORTY. We might try.

The YOUNG NUN. You shall not try. This shall not be told.

The ELDERLY NUN. But—a man . . .

The NUN of FORTY. No man could possibly be admitted here.

The ELDERLY NUN. I have seen a cardinal turned from our door.

The AGED NUN. I have seen a pope repulsed. The Abbess admitted him, yes; but she veiled her face and answered only with yes and no.

The YOUNG NUN (*as the sound rings louder*). You shall not tell. Indeed, you cannot tell. And even if you could I would not let you tell.

The AGED NUN. You are a rebellious spirit. How came you to seek these walls?

The YOUNG NUN. Have you ever heard of a headstrong pride?

The AGED NUN. I have.

The Young Nun. Do you know what lengths it may lead one to?

The Aged Nun (*humbly*). I fear not.

The Young Nun. Then you would not understand. (*Suddenly, to the* Nun *of* Forty.) Could you?

The Nun of Forty. I came from a mountain village. *He* was cruel to me. My parents, when they learned, were hardly less so. The whole little town turned against me; and I was glad to enter here. Pride? The best of those poor folk cannot over-indulge in pride; and I—I was not one of the best.—I could not understand.

The Young Nun. Then we will let it pass. — I was no village girl; the whole of a wide city rang with my name. I was only twenty when I came here. I lived within these walls five years. So that I am only twenty-five to-night. As for my fifteen years in the grave, they count for naught. I am still young and energetic, and I shake them off.

The Aged Nun. But I am seventy—perhaps eighty; for I lost all count long years before I died. I have no strength to throw off a single day.

The Young Nun. I lived here five years, I say — five raging, desperate years; yet I died in full possession of my senses. And I have kept them ever since.

The Nun of Forty. What caused your death?

The Young Nun. What caused my death? Never mind what caused my death — you shall not ask. They could not prove it! They could not prove it, I say!

The Nun of Forty. They tried to prove it. Not every one who departed under such a cloud could have hoped for rest in consecrated ground.

The Young Nun. We will not talk of clouds.— I died, as I say, in full possession of my senses; and, believe me, I have them with me even yet. *I* was not driven into

9

melancholia, like the poor soul who lies moaning now behind us on another's stone; *I* was not chained for twenty
years in a mad-cell, like the pitiful creature who crouches
gibbering yonder in the dark.

The ELDERLY NUN. Hush! such things are not to be
mentioned — not to be recalled.

[The air becomes closer. The luster of the moon begins to dim.]

The YOUNG NUN. I will recall others, then. First, let
me tell you one thing: while I was living here I saw the
whole sky — and more than once.

The NUN of FORTY. Impossible.

The YOUNG NUN. By no means. You think that all
the windows here are inner ones — that no single one looks
without. You are mistaken. There *is* one such window
— or was; secret, perhaps,— forgotten, possibly. I made
it mine. I saw the world. Not only the sky, but the sea
and the sea-shore for miles along, and the glow and fume
of the mountain, and the domes of the town below us, and
the ships in its harbor.

The NUN of FORTY. I never saw a ship.

The AGED NUN. I have long forgotten the sea.

The MELANCHOLY NUN. *He* was a sailor — a sailor.

The YOUNG NUN. One day I saw the harbor full of
black war-ships. I saw the smoke of their cannon. I saw
the town walls half battered down.

The ELDERLY NUN. What did that mean?

The YOUNG NUN. I do not know. I never learned.
I made it mean a thousand things. For I kept my wits
throughout, as I have told you.

The NUN of FORTY. I have kept mine, too.

The Young Nun. Such as they are.— Another day I saw the city draped in black. Processions of suppliants filed through the streets to the churches. I think there was a pestilence. I think that hundreds died — thousands. I thought of my mother — she was not to blame. I thought of my sister — she was, she was, she was! I wondered if they had fallen victims — of course I never learned. I thought of my lover —

The Nun of Forty. You had a lover, too?

The Young Nun. Yes.

The Nun of Forty. Was he cruel?

The Young Nun. As cruel as yours. But no more about him.

The Nun of Forty (*passionately, to the* Aged Nun). Why did *you* come here?

The Aged Nun. I have forgotten.

[The moon still dims. A sweeping flight of restless sea-birds passes overhead. The work on the wall proceeds, unheeded by the Nuns.]

The Young Nun. So, as you hear, I saw things. I could speculate — I could conjecture. Fasts were not enough for me, nor feasts, nor vigils. Flagellations were not sufficient to vary the monotony. It was not all in all if my linnet piped hoarsely —

The Elderly Nun. Do not touch on such themes. My poor thrush — I sorrowed over him for more than a month.

The Young Nun. It was not an event for me when I pricked my finger at sewing —

The Aged Nun. I have made an event out of less than that.

The YOUNG NUN. I lived upon observation and upon recollections. For I had moved in the great world, and I had many things to recall.

The ELDERLY NUN. I was only a toiler in the fields. I knew trees, cattle, toil, hunger — little else. There was not much to see; there was even less to remember.

The YOUNG NUN. Then let me tell you. Imagine a beautiful day in early spring, and a parade of carriages along the broad sea-front. Carriages and horses alike garlanded with flowers, and multitudes more of flowers flung from hand to hand as the fête went on. With the man who was to marry me I drove thus before the eyes of the entire city and flung my roses broadcast with the rest. Roses, I say; nothing grows here save asphodels.— My sister was with us . . . he left me . . . he married her . . .

The NUN of FORTY. And then?

The YOUNG NUN (*with vehemence*). Ah, the plague! It was a welcome sight! But enough of that.— Were you ever in a theater?

The NUN of FORTY. A theater? I?

The ELDERLY NUN. No more than in a carriage.

The YOUNG NUN. Then let me tell you. I went for the last time just a week before I came here. I sat near him — again the whole town saw us. But why do I return to him? — A beautiful creature appeared upon the stage.

The ELDERLY NUN. What did she do?

The YOUNG NUN. She danced.

The NUN of FORTY. What did she wear?

The YOUNG NUN. Little enough. A breadth or two of gauze; and jewels.

The ELDERLY NUN. Ah, jewels, jewels!

The YOUNG NUN. Jewels, indeed; they were better than mine! She stood and spun upon one toe —

The NUN of FORTY. Why?

The YOUNG NUN. — as if she had no weight whatever — as if nothing in the world could be easier. It was delightful. I think I could have done it too, if I had but been put at it in time. And how she smiled!

The ELDERLY NUN. Why?

The YOUNG NUN. Why? She must have had her reasons. Could she have smiled at . . . ? But enough of that.— As I say, she smiled. So did I. I could always smile — (too readily, too ignorantly, perhaps); I had beautiful teeth. I have them yet. I can smile yet. Shall I?

The ELDERLY NUN (*coldly*). This is no place for smiles.

The YOUNG NUN. Perhaps you are right. But be that as it may, I am alive. And that is just. Dead in life: alive in death. And justice is all I ask.

[The sound of a stone falling upon other stones. The air grows more and more oppressive. The peak of the mountain glows with a kindling anger and its trail of smoke moves on with a darker and wider reach. The earth seems to shiver.]

The YOUNG NUN. Ah, he is advancing! I hear the wall give way.

The ELDERLY NUN. He should be stopped.

The YOUNG NUN. He shall not be stopped. I am curious; I am interested; I have my wits still, I tell you. I believe in him. But — whom has he come to steal away?

The ELDERLY NUN. To steal away? This must be told. I shall run to the Abbess.

The YOUNG NUN. Go, wake her; go try to tell her. Could she hear you? Could she see you?

[Another stone falls. The bats tumble about heedlessly in the murky moonlight. Half awakened land-birds flit hither and thither with wild cries of alarm. The convent belfry quivers from top to base, and its bells are rung — but not by human hands.]

The NUN of FORTY. I am stifling — stifling. The air of the grave is wholesomer than this. I will go back — I will find my tombstone and draw it over me again.

[The NEW LITTLE NUN, with a cry of terror, starts from her corner and rushes out into the edge of the moonlight: a hand has been thrust through the gap in the wall and a voice has followed.]

The VOICE. Bianca! Bianca!
The NEW NUN. It is Angelo! It is Angelo!

[The NUNS advance toward her. It were vain to say (from her own terror and from the failing light) whether or no she hears them or sees them.]

The YOUNG NUN. This, then, it is whom he has come to steal away. Dear child, dear child! — do any of you know her?
The ELDERLY NUN. She is later than our time. She is far too young.
The NUN of FORTY. I think she is but newly come.
The YOUNG NUN (*motioning*). Child, child, go with him! Go, or you too may one day be glad to drink . . .
The NUN of FORTY. Ah! that is how you died! I knew it! I knew it! And yet you dared to take your place among us others who—

The YOUNG NUN. Go, child! Do not stop for the poison, the flagellations, the straps and chains of the mad-cell! — Does she hear me? — Does she hear me? — What did she answer him? Tell me, tell me!

The ELDERLY NUN. She only called him by name; she called him Angelo.

The YOUNG NUN. Angelo? *His* name! Let me advance; let the moon but shine out; let me only see his face! 'T is he, 't is he! — But no; that is impossible. And yet —

The NUN of FORTY. You recognize him?

The YOUNG NUN. I know the face. And now — I know the voice. It is his son — his son! — O girl, beware!

ANGELO (*advancing through the opening*). At last! I have sought you for three long days.

BIANCA (*waving him back*). Leave me, leave me!

ANGELO. None of your friends could tell me where you were. None of your family *would* tell me.

BIANCA. What need to know? What need to know?

ANGELO. All the need in the world. I had no other need.

BIANCA. You left me once; now leave me forever. You have been faithless — cruelly faithless.

The YOUNG NUN. Faithless! It is in the blood! My child, beware!

ANGELO. I myself am but escaped from confinement. Your uncle —

BIANCA. It was my uncle who first warned me. I believed him; I believe him yet.

ANGELO. — and your cousins —

BIANCA. They warned the poor orphan too. And then they told me that you had gone; they told me that you would never come back to me . . .

ANGELO. It is your uncle and your cousins who have separated us.

BIANCA. But why?

ANGELO. Why? Could you bring your fortune with you here? To whom should it then fall but to them? I have been faithful.

The YOUNG NUN. Believe it, child, even if it is not true! Any fate rather than the one that awaits you here!

[A thick dun cloud, illumined by intermittent flashes of volcanic fire, fills the cloister, and the lashings and groanings of a terrified sea come to them from below. The foundation-walls of the convent are all a-tremble, and the bells ring in an uncontrollable frenzy. The NUNS grope through the smoke and the darkness to seek retreat in their graves: not one can find her own.]

ANGELO (*to* BIANCA). You must leave here with me at once.

BIANCA. How is that possible?

ANGELO. Where I have climbed up you can climb down.

BIANCA. It is so far . . . It seems so dizzy . . . The opening is so small . . .

The YOUNG NUN (*standing alone in the middle of the enclosure, whence she shouts with all her might, as she waves her garment with two wild arms*). Try, try! Use your own hands, girl, on those horrible stones! — If such a chance had ever come to me! (*But they do not see her through the whirling smoke, nor do they hear her above the thunderous noise.*)

ANGELO. Courage, courage!

The YOUNG NUN. Courage — yes; take all of mine!

[A violent shock of earthquake. The graves are completely upheaved and dismantled; the belfry totters; and the Abbess and her train fly screaming past the church-door just as the walls of the cloister are rent from top to bottom. Through the opening thus made one sees the toppling towers of the city and the confounded shipping of the port, and beneath the lifting smoke one views a score of burning villages upon the lava-swept mountain-side.]

ANGELO (*pointing to the cleft wall*). There lies our way.

[ANGELO and BIANCA pick their path through the wrecked and dismantled tombs, upon whose ruins the DEAD NUNS lie wailing, affrighted and disconsolate.]

The YOUNG NUN. My narrow home is ruined with the rest. I could not live in life; I cannot rest in death. Come, the whole world shall now be mine. I have many lost years to regain, and where could I make a beginning of greater promise? Henceforth I shall pluck not the asphodel, but the amaranth; my moonlight shall no longer be green, but rosy-red; and even the humblest of the paths I take shall be paved for me with shimmering rainbows.

[She treads a resolute way among the lamenting choir, and disappears in the pall of smoke as she follows ANGELO and BIANCA down the hillside.]

NORTHERN LIGHTS.

NORTHERN LIGHTS.

PERSONS.

Oscar Holme.
Hilda, his wife.
Their Two Children.

The Pastor.
The Doctor.
A Nurse.

A living-room in a villa overlooking the North Sea. Through the window one observes the budding greenery of early spring. In the open fireplace a brisk fire flames and flickers. To one side, a desk littered with papers. Upon the wall, a picture of Saint Lawrence roasting on his gridiron. Present: the Pastor and the Doctor.

———

The Doctor. You say that she has scarcely spoken a word for three days?

The Pastor. Not one—save now and then, in a fit of reviving petulancy.

The Doctor. Then I have indeed chosen an unfortunate time to pay my respects.

The Pastor. The friendly advances of a new neighbor —you have there your justification. Besides, she is always sure to make lost time good. (*He wipes his brow with his handkerchief.*)

The DOCTOR. You find it warm here ?   So do I—much too warm either for health or comfort.

The PASTOR. This is the last house in the neighborhood to give up a fire in the spring, and the first to renew it in the autumn.

The DOCTOR.   An open fire is sometimes cheerful.

The PASTOR. That is the reason she gives.

The DOCTOR. They burn fagots, I see.

The PASTOR. And sometimes other things.   I have known her to burn her husband's manuscripts—and her children's toys.

The DOCTOR (*taking up a book from center-table*).   She is something of a reader, I judge; the wife of a literary man . . .

The PASTOR. By no means.   Books annoy her, rather; they irritate her; a dull book of just the right sort will sometimes drive her frantic.   She is so easily bored; she is a mere bundle of nerves.

The DOCTOR. Yet this book appears to contain her signature : " Hilda Holme, Brussels, October 10th."

The PASTOR. She brought it back home with her.

The DOCTOR. It is entitled : " The Great Conflagrations of History "; here is a leaf turned down at the Fire of London.   London—she must have found much to interest her in that great capital.   What a privilege to visit it !—one that I may never enjoy, I fear.

The PASTOR. On the contrary,—it depressed her; then it began to wear upon her—she declares that it almost drove her insane.   The thick air weighed upon her; the uproar of traffic racked her nerves . . . As to visiting foreign capitals—well, why should one attempt to become a cosmopolite?   Should not one rather remain national, provincial, even parochial, above all individual ?   To be individual, to assert one's own personality — ah, you have it there.

The Doctor. I know your views.— And here is another book, also hers: "Travels among the Fire-worshipers of Persia." And a third: "The Book of Martyrs" . . . This is really very —

The Pastor. Leave it. She comes.

[Enter Mrs. Hilda Holme, a pale, slender young woman with active eyes, a drawn face, and long, thin fingers which she works interlacingly. She is apparently passing from one mood to another, and the presence of visitors seems to help the transition.]

The Pastor. We are glad to see you, my dear Hilda, and to find you better. Here we have Doctor Kjoldmann, and we must greet him with the friendliness that such a new-comer deserves.

Hilda (*with a slow hesitation*). You are welcome, sir. (*She looks ahead rather vacantly, and her hands continue wrestling with each other.*) My husband is away from home, but he will be back presently.

The Doctor. You return improved, madam, after your long tour abroad?

Hilda. Return? Abroad? But that was many years ago; ten — fifteen; twenty, for aught I know.

The Pastor. No more than five, I swear.

Hilda. Five? It seems like fifty. There were no babies then. To have careered through the world as I once did, and then to end in this dull and obscure hole! — no society save that of books and dingy manuscripts; a husband with his nose constantly in his ink-pot; two children to wash and dress and dose . . . (*She turns her back and stares out through the window.*)

The DOCTOR. Madam, you malign our town, I am sure.

The PASTOR. You do indeed. It is an important place, I assure you. It is the center of the world — if you but choose to believe it. I *do* believe it.

The DOCTOR. Ah, that is right. We should believe in ourselves and in our own importance. Yet, the pleasure and the improvement incident to travel — the parks, the galleries, the churches, the hospitals, the castles, the theaters . . .

HILDA (*turning back, and with a certain animation*). Do not think it. Such things are wearying past all belief. Those Florentine galleries — I walked through them for miles. Not one of their pictures pleased me, save the original of that. (*She indicates the Saint Lawrence.*) How those red flames flicker and sting! How they light up the whole dark hall! How they take hold upon those shrinking limbs! — What is so beautiful as a fire? Let me show you! (*She throws another fagot upon the hearth.*)

The DOCTOR (*wiping his face*). If you do not care for painting, then, there is the stage. Think of the great theaters of Berlin, Paris, Vienna . . .

HILDA. I have seen them all — there is nothing more tiresome. Their comedies, their ballets! I know their parks, their grottoes, their pavilions. In all my tour but one spectacle really pleased me.

The DOCTOR. What was that?

HILDA. We were at Dresden. We went to the opera house. A woman in armor was laid to sleep upon a bed of rocks. Suddenly flames sprang up and encompassed her — their glare filled the whole stage. Something impelled me to my feet, and I felt a wild cry rising to my lips. "She will burn!" I was about to scream exultingly; "and we shall burn; and the whole house will burn!" But Oscar pulled me back; and then the curtain fell. A—ah!— Shall you mind if I smoke? (*She lights a cigarette.*)

The PASTOR. But, Hilda, this is not usual; this is not —not . . .

HILDA. I know you don't like it. Neither does Oscar. I do a good many things he does n't like—he is something of a prig. But to have a touch of smoke and flame just under your nose is really quite delightful. I recall those Russian princesses at Cannes; I ought to have been a princess too. Why do you look so—so . . .? What should I have under my nose, then? An ink-pot?

The PASTOR. But, my dear Hilda—

HILDA. But, my dear Pastor—you who are always standing out for individuality. Really, really, you must allow me to be myself, I think. (*She holds the match-box in her lap and lights match after match as the talk goes on.*)

The PASTOR. It is quite true that one should strive for the preservation of one's own individuality—

HILDA. Just as *you* have done, my dear Pastor! You are precisely like the pastor in the next town, and the next, and the next beyond that—

The PASTOR. But my case is different, child. I have my professional position and reputation to consider, and besides—

The DOCTOR. Besides, what would be the worth of a guide-post that followed up its own pointings?

HILDA. I have been no guide-post, thank heaven!

The PASTOR. But your children . . .

HILDA. Bother!

The DOCTOR. No guide-post, indeed, could have gone to Rome, to Paris, to Naples . . .

10

HILDA. Do not mention those tedious places, I beg you!

The DOCTOR. How, madam? You are not happy at home, you are not pleased abroad? What would you have? Where would you be?

HILDA. I do not know; I look for a somewhere that I have never seen—a something that I have never had.—Even in Paris itself I found nothing—nothing but a Panorama: the Burning of the City by the Commune. But that alone was enough. How the flames soared! how the roofs crashed! how the sky shone! how the sparks flew!

The DOCTOR. A fine work of art, no doubt.

HILDA. Let us not talk of works of art; let us speak of works of nature—of the real thing. Ah, the Girandola at Rome — what a grand spectacle after a month of delving amidst ruins and of prowling amongst churches! It was Oscar who delved and prowled—and I was dragged about with him. But that one heavenly night — the last of our stay—repaid me for all the rest. The flights of rockets that rose from the round mass of Sant' Angelo — the curving lines of light, the fiery showers of sparks! For one brief hour I lived. I danced and shrieked — I was myself. Can one shriek here? Can one dance here? No, no, no; one may mope here and mend one's children's frocks.

The DOCTOR. As you say, madam, you may recall the beauties of nature. You have beheld the Mediterranean, the Alps, the Bay of Naples, the Blue Grotto . . .

HILDA. Naples—it was a weary wilderness. The Blue Grotto — it froze my marrow. There was really nothing —except Pompeii and Vesuvius. Ah, Vesuvius!—what an experience! To tiptoe over half-cold lava crusts — to choke amidst the fumes of sulphur! To stand on the brink of the crater, enjoying the smoke, the rumblings, the showers

of red hot stones! On the edge of the great crater stood
a little one, hardly taller than a child; mother and baby!
And the little one fumed and sputtered and threw up its
tiny hot pebbles — all just like its elder. It was charming
— fascinating!

[Two children burst suddenly into the room. A Nurse
follows.]

HILDA. Ah, Grethe! Ah, Eric! Come to mamma;
stand at mamma's knee. Love mamma before these
strange gentlemen.— Why, what is it I smell? Whose
clothes have been burning?

ERIC (*in a nervous fright*). Mine, mamma.

HILDA. Dear me, dear me! — this poor little tunic all
scorched round the hem! And what are these marks on
your wrists?

ERIC. Ropes, mamma.

GRETHE. I had to tie him, mamma; he would n't stand
still.

The NURSE. Please, ma'am, I found him fastened to the
plane-tree in the garden, with a lot of chips heaped up
round his feet.

GRETHE. He was a martyr, mamma. I was just about
burning him alive, but he broke away.

HILDA. For shame, Eric! Why could n't you have
played prettily with your sister?

ERIC (*with a frightened sob*). I did, mamma; I —

The NURSE. Indeed he did, ma'am. He stood there
like a little lamb, until —

HILDA. I know his sullen fits. And these absurd and
annoying panics. Come, my poor Grethe, you and
mamma will build a nice little fire of our own right here

on the corner of the hearthstone, and nobody shall put it out, either. (*To the* DOCTOR.) I remember our last town fête, and how they extinguished the bonfire in the street before it had half burned itself out. Oh, that water!— it saddened me; it half sickened me. (*She starts a small fire at the corner of the hearthstone.*) We often do this. Oscar does n't like it, but we do it. Ah, my dears, how nicely it blazes! There, naughty Eric, you don't deserve all this kindness from good mamma, do you? But she forgives you, so don't be sulky and sullen. What! do you throw yourself on the floor? do you clutch at your own windpipe? Oh, fie!

The PASTOR. There is no danger here?

HILDA. Not a particle. You are thinking of our last Christmas tree. Well, we put it out, didn't we?

The DOCTOR. Pardon me, madam; but this abnormal . . .

HILDA. Abnormal dullness? I fear you are right. Oscar does so little to entertain us. We must do what we can to entertain ourselves. Martyrs at the stake!—a deliciously absurd idea, wasn't it?—There, my dears, you may watch the little fire a moment longer, and then you may go up stairs with Elspeth.

GRETHE. Oh, no, mamma!

HILDA. Well, then, just one more grand flare. What shall we burn?—let me see. Ah, to be sure! Run, Eric; bring me some of those sheets on papa's desk. Yes, from that thick pile; he can spare us a few as well as not. That 's right; rumple them, crumple them. What a beautiful little blaze!—The rest of them? Oh, throw them into the fireplace.—And now that 's all. Go with Elspeth, my dears; Elspeth will find something to amuse you.

[The NURSE starts to leave, with the two children.]

HILDA. My Grethe is so clever. No sooner do I read
her a page from the Book of Martyrs than she puts it into
practice. Eric is so different. I often wonder that two
children so dissimilar should be the offspring of the same
mother. Yet he and I are alike in some things. I have
yawned at weddings, and often I am bored to desperation
at the play. Oscar, now, is always about the same; what
could be more irritating? There are days when he and
his work and his quiet (he *must* have quiet) almost drive
me to frenzy.— Oh, Elspeth; before you leave, just light
the lamp.

The PASTOR. My dear Hilda, there still remains a good
half hour of daylight. [ELSPETH lights the lamp.]

HILDA. I know, I know. But the flame shines so beau-
tifully through the red shade.

[ELSPETH and the children go out.]

The DOCTOR. I fear we must be withdrawing . . . You
will convey my best respects to your husband . . .

HILDA. Don't go just yet; the lamp is only my whim.
You must not leave without meeting Oscar; he will be
along presently. Don't go — you have hardly bored me
at all. Besides, I have something to say to you.

The PASTOR. Shall *I* go, Hilda?

HILDA. Never mind. I shall not say that you have
not bored me, but as you are here you may as well stay on.

The DOCTOR. You have something to say to me?

HILDA. About myself, yes. I mean to be thoroughly
individual; I will talk about myself.

The PASTOR. That is a good beginning.

HILDA (*to the* DOCTOR). You have heard my remarks
about Oscar and the children and our life here. Now I
am going to tell you something else. What could be more
original, more individual, than to bestow confidences upon
a complete stranger?

The DOCTOR. You have my best attention.

HILDA. Well, then, what I have to tell you is this: I don't know who I am.

The PASTOR. You will yet find your true self.

HILDA. Nonsense!—I don't mean that. I mean I don't know my real name—I don't know who my parents were. I may suspect—I may have taken steps to learn; but I don't know.

The PASTOR. You are the daughter of Councilor Stockmann—everybody knows that.

HILDA. Everybody professes to know that. But such is by no means the real truth. The Councilor adopted me, and there the matter has rested, without comment or inquiry. I certainly passed my childhood at the Councilor's—a much livelier house than this, by the way—but I remember an earlier home and a different one. I think I left it suddenly one night. I think it was in flames. Oscar has gone to find out.

The DOCTOR. Your husband has gone to find out?

HILDA. I mean that he has gone into town for the day's mail. He will bring me back some books and papers, I think, that will help to clear matters up; I wrote for them a week ago. I believe we should try to understand things and ourselves and one another.

The PASTOR. Genealogy is worthy of our best attention.

The DOCTOR. And heredity too.

HILDA. Heredity,—precisely. You might think Grethe the last of a long line of inquisitors—or of incendiaries, and Eric the son of a—well, of a sentinel driven desperate by an endless succession of interminable guard-mounts and of a nun forced into moping melancholy by the tedium of the cloister. How will the coming generation end? Do you prophesy a quiet lapse into Nirvana or a sudden

catastrophe with all the trappings of tragedy ?   I shall attempt to decide as soon as Oscar arrives with my documents.   (*She looks out into the garden.*)   Here he comes
at last, and he has my packets too.   He does n't know
what they are ; besides, he is thinking about his own do-
ings.   (*She lights another cigarette.*)   Now you are going
to hear all about the Civilization of the Etruscans.

[Enter HOLME, a grave, self-contained young man, with
several parcels.]

HILDA. Oscar, you know the Pastor, and he will make
you acquainted with our new neighbor, Doctor Kjoldmann.
You might have come sooner.   You have some books for
me, and letters, and documents ; let me take them.   Gentlemen, I leave you.   I am meaning henceforth to do
largely as I please, and it is necessary for me to learn, as
a beginning, how far I can go.   (*She passes out.*)

OSCAR. Excuse, gentlemen, my delayed return.   Yet I
apprehend your welcome to have been a warm one : this
fire, this lamp ; even my wife's . . .   (*He pulls a bell-cord ;*
ELSPETH *appears.*)   Scatter the fire, Elspeth ; open the
window and draw wide the curtains ; put out the lamp —
no, let that remain as it is ; the darkness is overtaking us —
I see the first stars.   So.—And where are the children?

The NURSE. They are playing in the nursery.

OSCAR. They are in no mischief?

The NURSE. I think not, sir.

OSCAR. Very well.   (*The* NURSE *goes.*)   Even my wife,
as I was saying . . .

The PASTOR. My dear Oscar, believe that her reception
of us was all that it should have been.   I have seldom
seen her more sprightly, more—ah-um . . .

OSCAR. You relieve me. To rescue her from the gulf of black despondency into which she is sure to find herself plunged after one of her inexplicable nervous crises . . . (*To the* DOCTOR.) You will pardon these domestic details? . . .

The DOCTOR. Assuredly.

OSCAR. I sometimes believe that we are too quiet here, too absorbed in ourselves. I think now and then of a change—Italy again. (*To the* DOCTOR.) Does n't it seem to you that . . . ?

The DOCTOR. I am hardly prepared to advise . .

OSCAR. True—not yet, not now. But sometime I may be glad to have your opinion on . . .

The DOCTOR. At your service, I am sure.

OSCAR. Italy—yes. My first book, The Memories of the Cattegat, made our Italian trip possible. My second, From Præstöe to Palermo, built this house. A feat, you think? By no means. Two or three thousand copies selling at two or three crowns, and then the villa—what could be simpler, or commoner? My third book (*glancing toward desk*), The Etruscan Civilization, may pay our way across the Alps once more.—Oh, fie! what a smudge Elspeth has raised! The whole house might be thought to be filled with smoke!

[He opens the window still wider, and draws the curtains yet farther apart. From the horizon-line of the sea the Aurora Borealis streams and quivers in the deepening blue of the evening sky.]

OSCAR. Hilda was always my inspiration. My first book was written during my courtship, and sometimes she held the pens. The second was planned during our honeymoon. No book, my dear Doctor, can be written without feminine inspiration — that is the invariable rule..

The Doctor. And your new work — has it been long under way?

Oscar. Three years. I have done it largely alone. (*Quickly.*) It calls for less inspiration, but for more research, more industry. Yes, three years of close thought and application. (*He glances toward his desk with an impatience but half concealed.*)

The Pastor. Night is falling. We will take our leave.

The Doctor. With our best wishes for the prosperity of you and yours.

[They go out. As they leave by one door, enter Hilda by another. She has an open letter in one hand and a book in the other.]

Hilda. The whole thing is as clear as day — and substantially what I have long supposed. It seems that my grandfather — They have gone, have they?

Oscar. One moment, Hilda. What is the meaning of this outrageous fire, and of these charred papers on the hearth, and of the cigarette you had between your teeth as I came in? You know my objection to your smoking even in private, while to smoke before strangers —

Hilda (*with a staccato-like coldness*). Listen, Oscar. Henceforth you will take a different tone with me. I know at last just who I am. I shall be hectored and browbeaten no longer. From now on, you will bear this in mind: that my great-grandfather was an historical character, and that my grandmother on the other side —

Oscar. I have known all this from the beginning.

HILDA. You have known all this from the beginning! Then your lack of deference is quite inexplicable.

OSCAR. Indeed?

HILDA. Have a care, Oscar; I give you fair warning. Remember that my father's grandfather never sat at home writing miserable books. No; he was a leader of men. How many of these valleys did he devastate with fire and sword! How many villages and farmhouses went up in flames as he and his soldiers swept by! How many times the sky was reddened with — !

OSCAR. I should make no boast of that.

HILDA. Then recall my grandmother, the sainted Lady of Lindegaard, who founded a lay sisterhood and passed a long widowhood in fasts and prayers and contemplations . . .

OSCAR. There are better things than that to do.

HILDA. What better things? To dabble in an ink-pot? To snow one's self under, leaf by leaf, with endless manuscripts? Oscar, you never married me; you married that desk. Grethe and Eric are not your children; your children are the Cattegat and the — the ancient Etruscans!

OSCAR. My children are worthier of boast than your forebears. Hear me: your grandfather was apprehended for arson; he burnt his neighbors' houses — one night he even burnt his own. Over the very heads of his family. On that night your own life was barely saved.

HILDA. Ah!

OSCAR. And now, your sainted grandmother. Totally misunderstanding her own nature, she drove herself mad by a long life of puritanical futilities, and was more than half suspected of having done herself to death in the millpond.

HILDA. And you have never mentioned these things before?

OSCAR. Are they things one would willingly recall?

HILDA (*meditatively*). Well, then, there are two ways open to me. But I shall never go to the mill-pond. That would be too wet.

OSCAR. What are you saying, Hilda?

HILDA. Only this: I shall do something, sometime, Oscar. That would be the only end for a long life with you — the man who set his bride of a fortnight to measuring Etruscan tombs! — Pah! this smoke *is* thick — beyond all reason. (*She steps to the window. The* NORTHERN LIGHTS *flaunt brilliantly above the sea.*) Ah, see them, see them,— the only thing that reconciles me to life in this odious corner. They are a part of me, and I of them. They are the brands wielded by my ancestors of a hundred generations ago. The great gods have bestirred themselves, and they are setting the world afire. *You* will never set the world afire, Oscar!

OSCAR (*who, heedless of* HILDA'S *words, has turned his attention to his manuscripts*). Who has been at this desk? Who has been among my papers?

HILDA (*leaving the window*). Is anything amiss?

OSCAR. I miss a hundred sheets or more. What has been done with them? What are those charred papers upon the hearth-stone?

HILDA. We built a little fire there — the children and I.

OSCAR. Why? (*With a nervous dread.*) Fire, fire, always fire!

HILDA. Why? For our own pleasure. I'm sure we have little enough.

OSCAR. Built a fire? With what?

HILDA. Just with some loose papers from your desk. Were they of any value?

OSCAR. Of any value? Woman, woman, what have

you done? My last and greatest work — three years of thought and study — reduced to a handful of ashes! You are indeed your grandfather's — Leave me, leave me! Out of my sight!

HILDA. Have a care, Oscar. I warn you. I *am* his grandchild — I shall not go to the mill-pond! (*She advances toward the fireplace and begins to scatter the red embers over the hearth-rug and the floor.*)

OSCAR. Stop, stop! Are you mad? — mad with the madness of your race!

[Reënter, in breathless haste, the PASTOR and the DOCTOR.]

The PASTOR. Pardon me; something is much amiss.

The DOCTOR. Smoke is issuing through your roof; a red glare shines through all your upper windows!

The PASTOR. We saw it from the roadway, just as we were turning the last corner.

HILDA. And the Aurora — did you notice that, as well? When has it ever been more brilliant? When has it ever streamed up more magnificently? Oh, if there were but a torch in my hand too!

[Enter, hastily, the NURSE.]

The NURSE. Oh, master, master! The house is burning! The children must have built a fire upon the nursery floor!

OSCAR. Must have? Must have? What do you mean? Have you deserted them? Come, come! (*He rushes frantically toward the doorway.*)

The NURSE. Their door was fastened. I heard them screaming.

OSCAR. Oh, heavens!

HILDA (*with a shriek of triumph*). Ha! What did I tell you? They were not your children, but mine—they would not go to the mill-pond either!—A torch, a torch—I would give the world for a torch! (*She crosses over to the lamp.*) Give me two—one for each hand! Give me twenty—give me a hundred! (*She seizes the lamp.*) Wait, Oscar.—You have never seen me lovelier. You have never appreciated me—you have thought only of that desk. And now it is too late—I am forever beyond your reach. (*To the* PASTOR *and the* DOCTOR.) Go, you wretched prosers, go; it is you and your likes that have helped to drive me upon my fate! (*They move toward the doorway.*) And—now!

[She swings the lamp in a fiery circle round her head, then hurls it violently into the midst of her husband's desk, where it explodes. In an instant the room, with everything in it, is flecked and spotted with a spray of blazing oil. At the same time, flames burst through the ceiling.]

HILDA (*on fire, as she runs round and round the room*). Life is too dull to live; this is the only true way to die!

[The room fills with thick smoke, and the fate of the remaining personages is left altogether to surmise.]

THE STORY-SPINNER

THE STORY-SPINNER.

PERSONS.

The WAYFARER.	The BRIDEGROOM.
The BRIDE.	His PARENTS.
Her PARENTS.	His UNCLE.
Her GRANDMOTHER.	Many guests, servitors, musi-
An Old NURSE.	cians, etc.

The pleasance in front of the manor-house of Belcaro. It is laid out upon a hillside and affords a view, over some miles of undulating olive groves, of the towers of a medieval Tuscan town and of the mountains beyond and round about it. Immediately adjoining this boxed and laureled pleasure-ground is the doorway of a Romanesque chapel. A bell is ringing.— Present: the NURSE and the WAYFARER.

———

The NURSE. I cannot conceive why I should be speaking so freely of these things to you—to you, an utter stranger.

The WAYFARER. I enjoy such confidences, believe me. They are more grateful to me than the plentiful cheer of the servants' quarters or even the lordly dishes of the great banquet-hall itself.

The NURSE. I have never spoken of these matters to a

11   161

human soul before. I feel that I should have spoken earlier, or not at all.

The WAYFARER. Continue freely. What you say adds
nothing to my burden, yet lightens yours. What is one
more little tale to a man who has lived so long, traveled so
far and heard so much?

The NURSE. What prompts me to tell you all so freely?
It is not your gray hair — for mine is as gray as yours. It
is not your commanding mien — for tall and self-willed men
have never been strangers in this house. Is it perchance
your eye? It glitters with the knowledge of many things
far, far beyond my ken, and its questionings call forth answers that may not be withheld.

The WAYFARER. Go on.

The NURSE. I have no choice. — The loss of the first
child could bring me no single jot of blame; the loss of the
second, so soon after the disappearance of the other, might
well have been my ruin. The boy — Belcaro's heir though
he be — was no charge of mine; the girl was, and in the
strictest sense. That the boy should have been carried off
by bandits and that he should have disappeared so suddenly and so completely from among them upon the very
day that the ransom was ready to be paid — all this grieved
me, for he was a beautiful child and the sole heir of our
house. But *my* skirts were clear — *my* hands were clean.
Yet, when —

The WAYFARER. When, a year later, their infant daughter was lost as well . . .

The NURSE. I *was* to blame. Yet if ever there were
excuse . . . ! This house was attacked at night. We
fled — the chances of war. The babe and I were separated from its parents. I plunged frantically into the
wood, with that week-old child; all was dark, save for our

burning roofs. I hid the child and sought long for food
and shelter. These I found at length — but the child,
never. I groped my way back toward her — I searched
vainly for the spot. I saw her no more; I did not see
her parents for a year. Then the wars were over; our
household was once more gathered together. I returned,
too. And I brought a child with me.

The WAYFARER. What child?

The NURSE. One that I begged from a band of gipsies
— one that they had stolen, doubtless.

The WAYFARER (*thoughtfully*). This is most promising
— most promising. — And the other child? Nothing was
ever heard of it?

The NURSE. By me alone. Years after. A baby's skel-
eton, found where I could not find the baby itself.

The WAYFARER. So that the girl who is to be married
to-day is not the daughter of her reputed parents?

The NURSE. No more than the youth who is to marry
her is the son of his reputed parents.

The WAYFARER. Not their son? Not the heir of Montegrifone?

The NURSE. Only by adoption, I am told. The master
of Montegrifone (you see his walls across the valley) had
lately lost all his children through the plague. He re-
sorted to the monastery of which one of his brothers was
the head (you see its roofs upon the mountain-slope above),
where he found a young boy lodged for the time being.
The boy was handsome and clever and the lonely father
adopted him for his own. That was years ago, and for
his own he passes. You follow all this?

The WAYFARER. Readily. I see the most striking possibilities here. Proceed — proceed!

The NURSE. Proceed? Have I not said enough? That

night in the forest — the loss of my charge — that year of remorseful wanderings— that bartering with the gipsy band — the odious and lasting lies that followed my return — the finding, years after, of those little bones — the death of all those other innocents from the pestilence — Is not that enough?   Are you insatiable?

The WAYFARER. I am fond of a good story — that is all.

The NURSE. A good story! — have you no more than that to say? You are unfeeling. You are inhuman. I hold no further speech with you!

The WAYFARER. Go on; you interest me deeply. It is upon such things as these that I live.

The NURSE. I have no more to tell you. The rest you must see for yourself.

The WAYFARER. Is it true that these two families have been enemies for many generations?

The NURSE. Judge from their actions as they come to chapel.

The WAYFARER. Is it true that the bride's grandmother is still opposed to this marriage?

The NURSE. She has not forgotten the murder of her husband.

The WAYFARER. Is it not a fact that the uncles of the bridegroom — ?

The NURSE. They were balked in their attempt to hold this place as their own.

The WAYFARER. And is it not certain that — ?

The NURSE. Cease, cease, I pray you. There is more knowledge in your questions than in my answers even. I have told you too much; I have spoken far too freely. Who are you?

The WAYFARER. One who is fond of a good story — nothing more.

[The Bridal Party appears, accompanied by guests, musicians and the retainers of the castle, and moves along slowly toward the door of the Chapel.]

The BRIDE'S FATHER (*to the* GROOM'S FATHER). It is on such a day as this that I most envy you; it is on such a day that you should most sympathize with me. Save for the foray of those accursed freebooters I too should have a son to-day to follow me in good time and to serve as the future mainstay of my house.

The GROOM'S FATHER. Believe me when I say that no less do I envy you your daughter. We take her to-day because we are entitled to her; she will replace the baby girl that the gipsies spirited away from us so many years ago: a moment's inadvertence — rued so long and never recompensed till now.

The BRIDE'S FATHER. Yes, I remember. We were fellows in misfortune.

The WAYFARER (*to the* NURSE). Did you know this? Why did you withhold it? Did you not know that the daughter of Montegrifone had been stolen by a gipsy band?

The NURSE. I profess neither knowledge nor ignorance. I have said too much.

The WAYFARER. You have kept back essential facts, vital facts. You have not said enough.

The NURSE. I am under no obligation to disclose them.

The WAYFARER. I shall know how to punish you.

The NURSE. Ha! will you break your word? — But what, man, is all this to you? Why do your eyes glow? Why does your breath quicken? Why do you tug so at your interlocking fingers?

The WAYFARER. I am one who is fond of a good story.

And I am always on the side of youth and love and beauty.

[The Bridal Procession has reached the entrance of the Chapel. As it is about to pass through, the BRIDE's GRANDMOTHER appears from within.]

The BRIDE's GRANDMOTHER. Hold! I cannot find it in me to let this thing go farther.

The BRIDE's FATHER. I beg, mother, that you will no longer oppose. The past is past; old feuds are to be forgotten; this day will wipe out all differences between Montegrifone and Belcaro.

The GROOM's FATHER. Madam, I say the same. This will be the dawn of a new day for all of us. Do nothing more to prevent this union. Concede that such a youth as this my son is well worthy of even such a maiden as your granddaughter.

The WAYFARER (aside to the Nurse). He speaks truly. His son seems indeed a noble and gallant youth, and your young charge, in point of grace and beauty, appears fully worthy of him. My heartiest sympathies go with them both.

The BRIDE's GRANDMOTHER. You ask too much. Am I to forgive your brothers' attack upon our walls? Am I to forget our blazing roofs, my murdered husband?

The WAYFARER (stepping forward with an air of great dignity and authority). A word, madam. Do you not know that it was to this man's intercession with his brothers that you owed the preservation of your home and the final restitution of your property?

The BRIDE's FATHER. Is this indeed true?

The GROOM's FATHER (gulping down an instinctive

word of negation). Would such have been more than a mere act of justice and humanity?

The BRIDE'S FATHER. Then, madam my mother, let us and our children pass. Such an act cements a lasting friendship.

[The BRIDE'S GRANDMOTHER, still unreconciled, withdraws into the shadow of the doorway.]

The NURSE (*aside to the Wayfarer*). Is this thing true? The WAYFARER. It may be. It should be.

[A hasty step, accompanied by the clicking of armor and the jangling of swords, is heard. Enter the GROOM'S UNCLE, followed by several attendants.]

The GROOM'S UNCLE. Let this folly cease — it has gone too far already. We are enemies — we always have been — we always shall be. As such I came here once before; as such I come here now.

The BRIDEGROOM. Peace, uncle. You can have no voice in this. All has been decided. The past is past . . .

The GROOM'S FATHER. Peace, Bertuccio. Let those old memories die.

The WAYFARER. Peace, indeed. Do you not understand (*to the Uncle*) why you find yourself free to come to this place to-day? Do you not sometimes wonder that such a career as yours should be proceeding in broad sunlight instead of in the darkness of the dungeon? Recall the day when you were apprehended for your many acts of dishonor and violence. Do you know who appeared before the Great Council to plead your cause?

The GROOM'S UNCLE. No one, I trust. I need no advocate.

The WAYFARER. You had one. It was the voice of this woman here (*indicating the* BRIDE'S MOTHER) that saved your liberty and perhaps your life.

The BRIDE'S FATHER. Is this true, Olivia?

The BRIDE'S MOTHER (*gasping weakly, under the fixed gaze of the Wayfarer*). He was my — Bertuccio was my — my cousin . . .

The BRIDE'S FATHER. Ay! But how many times removed!

The NURSE (*aside to the Wayfarer*). Is this thing true?

The WAYFARER. Was it impossible?

The GROOM'S UNCLE (*to the Wayfarer*). Who are you, man, thus to force so unwelcome a fact upon me? Why are you here? What motive prompts you?

The WAYFARER. I am but a poor plodder, my lord, along life's highway. It is my pleasure to view the world and the men and manners that make it up. To-day has brought its jugglers, its tumblers, its musicians, and it has brought — me.

The BRIDEGROOM. You are discordant, uncle. Tune yourself anew, or leave us.

[The BRIDE'S GRANDMOTHER suddenly reappears in the doorway, and sees the GROOM'S UNCLE.]

The BRIDE'S GRANDMOTHER. There he stands! I see him once again. His sword is in one hand; why is not his torch in the other? It was he who urged them on; it was he who made me a widow; it was he who would have sacked and wrecked my house! And yet you ask me to . . .

The WAYFARER (*to himself*). My hand is now in the

flames, indeed! (*To the* UNCLE, *with increased dignity.*)
Listen to me.

The GROOM'S UNCLE. Silence! I will not.

The WAYFARER. You must; you shall.— Recall the
great battle on the banks of the Ersa when all the forces
of the state united to repel the invader. You saved a life
that day.

The GROOM'S UNCLE. I took a hundred. I saved not
one. I never saved a life.

The BRIDE'S FATHER. *I* saved a life that day.

The WAYFARER (*with a quick adaptation*). Ay, to be
sure. You found a warrior weighted down by his own
armor, struggling desperately for his life amidst the mud
and rushes of the shore—

The BRIDE'S FATHER. —and drew him up in safety
upon firm ground.

The WAYFARER. And his name? His face?

The BRIDE'S FATHER. I did not see it—his helm was
down. But he was one of our men.

The GROOM'S FATHER (*to the* UNCLE). You were thus
saved that day, Bertuccio. Later I saw you fighting, beslimed from head to foot.

The WAYFARER (*instantly seizing the advantage*). You
were that man.

The GROOM'S UNCLE. I deny it! They beg for my
liberty, they give me my life, they force their friendship
upon me—! I will not endure it!

The NURSE (*to the* WAYFARER). Is this thing true?

The WAYFARER. It is possible. Men have been drowned
in their armor; men have been saved in a hurly-burly
without either recognition or thanks.

The BRIDE'S GRANDMOTHER (*to her son*). A worthy
deed! The next time raise the visor!

The WAYFARER (*to the* GROOM'S UNCLE).   Let me try once more.—Recall the great flood of the following year. At twilight the town bridge was broken down and swept away.   It was crowded with human beings —many women among them.   Did you leave those poor creatures to save themselves?

The GROOM'S UNCLE (*reluctantly*).   I rescued two or three.

The BRIDE.   Among them was — I.   With a hundred others I fell into the rushing torrent.   A strong swimmer seized me and bore me to the shore.   It was too dark to see his face.   He gave me no time to thank him, but straightway plunged into the flood to save another unfortunate.

The WAYFARER (*pointing to the* GROOM'S UNCLE). There stands your savior. ·

The GROOM'S UNCLE.   Man, man, you will drive me mad!

The NURSE (*to the* WAYFARER).   Is this thing true?

The WAYFARER.   Why do you doubt?   Many risked their lives that night; many poor souls were saved.

The GROOM'S UNCLE.   I will not acknowledge that I saved his daughter's life.   Nor will I acknowledge that he himself saved mine!

The BRIDE'S GRANDMOTHER.   Nor will I acknowledge that your brothers' intercession saved my life and lands, or that the pleadings of my daughter-in-law saved you from many lingering years of chains and dungeons.   I know why you were caught floundering in the river: you were crossing over to the enemy, and you richly deserved to drown — or worse.

The GROOM'S FATHER.   Madam, you go too far.   You may accuse my brother of much — and truly; but you shall not breathe of treachery on the field of battle.

The BRIDEGROOM. You have gone too far indeed. Montegrifone shelters no traitor. That word strikes not only at my uncle; it strikes at my father, and at me. Until it is withdrawn I cannot pass that door.

The BRIDE. You, Gerardo, who have been so calm and reasonable throughout! You, whose kin my father saved from death and my mother from prison . . .

The GROOM'S UNCLE. I deny it! I deny it. Tell me, woman (*to the* BRIDE'S MOTHER), did you ever make plea for me before the Great Council? Answer me truly.

The BRIDE'S MOTHER (*feebly*). N — no.

The GROOM'S UNCLE. Ha! There you have it!

The GROOM'S MOTHER. No more, then, did your husband save Bertuccio's life.

The BRIDE'S GRANDMOTHER. See, Ruggiero! What do they give you?— thanks — or the lie?

The GROOM'S FATHER. You accuse us of treachery, of falsehood?

The BRIDE'S FATHER. Of both; of worse. Of violence, of injustice, of —

The GROOM'S FATHER (*to the* BRIDEGROOM). Leave that girl's side.

The BRIDEGROOM. Do I need the word?

The BRIDE'S FATHER (*to the* BRIDE). Drop that man's hand.

The BRIDE. Have I not the pride of our house?

The NURSE (*to the* WAYFARER). The fault is yours. You have gone too far; you have said too much.

The WAYFARER. I shall go much farther. I shall say much more.

The GROOM'S UNCLE (*to the* BRIDE'S FATHER). Draw and defend yourself.

The BRIDE'S FATHER. You find me ready.

[The Chapel bell goes on ringing. Two acolytes, sent to learn the reason for delay, stand upon the threshold in an attitude of amazed protest. More of the men draw their swords, and a general combat seems imminent, when the WAYFARER, his eye rolling in a fine frenzy, and his carriage full of dignity and authority, advances into the midst of the group.]

The WAYFARER. Hold! You are all groping in the darkness. Let me illumine it—that is my office. I cannot brook to see the happiness of this young couple wrecked by the blind folly of their elders. I ever side with youth and hope and beauty and courtesy and love; such are the things I live upon.

The GROOM'S UNCLE. You are a foolish meddler. Stand aside.

The WAYFARER. I must needs meddle where others muddle.

The BRIDE'S FATHER. You are a stranger. Let your discretion match with your ignorance.

The WAYFARER. A stranger—yes; ignorant—no. I tread the highways of the world; at times I wander through the byways as well. Give me your hand and I will lead you through them too. You lost a son?

The BRIDE'S FATHER. Years ago.

The WAYFARER. A band of robbers carried him off. (*To* GROOM'S FATHER.) You adopted a son?

The GROOM'S FATHER. Years ago,— a bright boy who had found temporary lodgment in a monastery where I had a family interest.

The WAYFARER. Well and good. The boy was brought there by one of the monks. The monk had received him at the hands of a robber chief. The robber, dying, confessed to the monk that the boy, the son of noble parents, had been stolen away by his own band. I was lodging in the monastery when the monk and his young charge arrived. I know that youth's whole history. He stands this moment between you, and he is the heir not of Montegrifone but of Belcaro—not your son, but *yours*.

The NURSE (*pointedly, to the* WAYFARER). You were lodging in that monastery ?

The WAYFARER (*sternly*). I was. Do not doubt it.

The BRIDEGROOM. What! Shall I be made the brother of . . . ?

The WAYFARER. No. (*To* GROOM'S FATHER.) I rob you of a son—a son by adoption. I replace him by a daughter—a daughter of your own flesh and blood. Recall that baby girl who was stolen by a band of gypsies. I knew them and their camp. One night a guilty nurse, who had lost the infant committed to her care, came to that camp and bargained for a child. The lost child was Belcaro's, and the child substituted for it was yours.

The NURSE (*to the* WAYFARER). You were dwelling in that gipsy camp ?

The WAYFARER (*menacingly*). I was. Do not question it.

The BRIDE. What! Must I believe myself the daughter of . . . ?

The WAYFARER (*in a fine glow of exaltation*). Now you know all. Well and good. Let the church-door close; let the bridal procession turn back; do what you may, undo what you can. But these facts remain: for twenty years and more, you (*to* MONTEGRIFONE) have fed and lodged and instructed Belcaro's son; and for twenty years or less you (*to* BELCARO) have cherished and protected Montegrifone's daughter. What can either of you do now that will undo all this ? [A pause.

The BRIDE'S FATHER. The bell is still ringing.

The GROOM'S FATHER. The door is still open.

The BRIDE'S GRANDMOTHER. I no longer oppose.

The GROOM'S UNCLE. I willingly submit.

The BRIDEGROOM. These varying heirships shall blend.

The BRIDE. These perplexing parentages must fuse.

The BRIDE'S MOTHER (*to the* WAYFARER). Pray join us in our festivities.

The GROOM'S MOTHER (*to her husband*). Such services as these must not be allowed to go unrecompensed.

The WAYFARER. The bell is ringing; the door is open; the priest is waiting. Pass in, pass in!

[The Bridal Procession enters the chapel. There remain outside only the WAYFARER and the NURSE.]

The NURSE (*after a long pause*). Who are you?

The WAYFARER. A poor plodder along life's highway. One whose pleasure it is to view the passing show — and to direct it, when such seems fit.

The NURSE. You have done great things to-day.

The WAYFARER. I have done greater. It is my office to smooth the rough places, to untangle the tangled skein.

The NURSE. What do you call yourself?

The WAYFARER. A fiction-monger — a story-spinner. I work in words when I must, but in deeds when I may; by tongue or pen when nothing better offers, in human heart-beats when the chance but comes my way.

The NURSE. You are leaving? You will not wait to see the bride come forth from the chapel?

The WAYFARER. My task here is finished.

The NURSE. You will not tarry to take your place in the banquet hall?—right bravely have you earned it!

The Wayfarer. The world is wide and other tasks await me in it.

The Nurse. But before you go, one word.

The Wayfarer. What is it ?

The Nurse. All these things,—are they—are they— true ?

The Wayfarer. They may be. They ought to be.— Farewell.   [He goes.

THE STRANGER WITHIN THE GATES

THE STRANGER WITHIN THE GATES

PERSONS.

The STRANGER.
The HOST of the GOLDEN OWL. (He is also BURGOMASTER.)
His DAUGHTER.

The COUNT of HABICHTSBURG.
His NIECE.
The WATCHMAN.
His WIFE.

Various TOWNSPEOPLE; among them: the SCHOOLMASTER, the PRIEST, the MASTER-BUILDER. Servants, Men-at-arms, etc.

A little square just within the gate of the town of Habichtsburg. On the right, the castle, which incorporates a portion of the town walls. On the left, the inn of the Owl. Opposite it, a fountain which half hides the entrance to the church. At a table under the great linden-tree before the inn are discovered the STRANGER, the HOST, the SCHOOLMASTER and various townspeople. Sunset; the sun shines through the town gate.

———

The STRANGER (*to the* SCHOOLMASTER). What you say interests me deeply;—me, one who is in no wise given to reflection.

The SCHOOLMASTER. I had hardly thought to produce so great an impression. What I have said can scarce be called novel;—it is not, indeed, my office to deal in novelties.

The STRANGER. You have not offered novelties. I have met all these ideas more than once before. But it is only the twentieth presentation that can make me think. I find again, then, some thousand souls dwelling in intimacy—in close space and with close interests. A permanent intimacy, too, as I understand, and one governed by various small rules and regulations that are in some degree of your own contriving. I myself am a person of action, and nothing else; yet when I encounter such conditions for the twentieth, the fiftieth, the hundredth time, it almost gives me food for thought.

The WATCHMAN. There are a hundred towns like this?

The STRANGER. Possibly, my good fellow; possibly. I myself have seen ten or twelve such—I will not go so high as twenty twice.

The HOST of the OWL. Which of the twenty is yours?

The STRANGER. Which of them is mine? This; decidedly, this.

The HOST. This? You are not enrolled here; you are not known here—not a soul of us has ever seen your face before.

The STRANGER. Denied welcome even here? Then am I homeless indeed. Will you not make me one of yourselves for a single night?

The PRIEST. That were but charity.

The STRANGER. One night — no more; one will be quite enough. For, if you tell me truly, life here is too beset by restrictions for comfort—to say nothing of pleasure. One may not be at liberty, for example, to kiss his neighbor's wife or daughter?

The HOST. I should like to see a man kiss my daughter!

The WATCHMAN. I should like to catch a man kissing my wife!

The STRANGER (*to the* HOST'S DAUGHTER, *who comes with a fresh flagon*). Thank your stars, my child, that you are so well protected. I shall have to look elsewhere. (*He casts up his eye and sees a young woman at a window above the town-gate.*) Toward you, my dear. (*He throws a kiss aloft.*)

The WATCHMAN. Have a care, young sir. That is my wife!

The STRANGER. That lovely young creature *your* wife? Who could have guessed it! (*The young woman blushes, smiles and retires.*)

The WATCHMAN. There is now no need to guess; you know.

The STRANGER. Thanks for the assurance, graybeard. —No endearments, then, are permitted. No more is one at liberty, I suppose, to put his hand into his neighbor's pocket?

The HOST. I should like to see any one put his hand into my pocket!

The MASTER-BUILDER. I should like to catch any one putting his fingers on my purse!

The HOST'S DAUGHTER (*to the* STRANGER, *at a sign from her father*). Your reckoning, sir.

The STRANGER (*carelessly*). Presently, presently, my dear child.

The HOST. At once, if you please.

The STRANGER. Your poor pocket!—button it, button it; lock the stable door!

The HOST. You will not pay?

The STRANGER. We shall reach that point in due time. One is not free, then, to filch. No more may one draw his blade, I conceive, to end an objectionable and super-fluous life? (*The* HOST *shrinks back.*)

The WATCHMAN. I should like to see anyone draw against—(*He pauses as he perceives his own pike dandled carelessly between the* STRANGER'S *knees.*)

The STRANGER. Oh, take it, take it—by all means!— Then I may not run you through and through, I may not hamstring you, I may not even pink you? No more would you allow me, I fancy, the right to lay the torch to yonder door. (*He points across toward the entrance to the castle.*)

The SCHOOLMASTER. What thoughts are yours!

The PRIEST. No one here dreams of so wicked a deed.

The HOST. Such an assault upon the sacred rights of property!

The WATCHMAN. Such an affront to law! Such an attack upon life!

The MASTER-BUILDER! Could you destroy in a moment of frenzy the thought of so many minds and the skill of so many hands through so many laborious years?

The GARDENER. Take, rather, my axe, and wreck in one hour the work of centuries by laying low the ancient linden under whose shade we rest.

The STRANGER. What, are you all so cramped and stiffened in your chains? Nothing for you save restric-tions . . . repressions . . . ?

The SCHOOLMASTER. We obey the laws.

The STRANGER. Mere habit—mere inertia; the numbing custom of generations.

The PRIEST. But the bonds of conscience . . . the ordi-nances of religion . . .

The STRANGER. Religion!—the special color cast by each age and race upon a matter that begins in fog and ends in conjecture!

The Host. The ties of family . . .

The Stranger. O, la, la!   What individual, left to his own devices, would ever hit upon matrimony and follow it in practice?

The Watchman. The rights of property, the security of—

The Stranger. Tush!   What property has the lion, the tomtit?   Each takes whatever he needs wherever he finds it.— But on these points are you unanimous?   Do you all obey?   Do you all conform?   Do you all observe the rules of the game?

The Priest. All.

The Schoolmaster. All.

The Stranger (*pointing toward the castle*).   All — absolutely all?   (*A pause.*)   Ah, no answer!— Hark, hark!   I think the answer comes.

[Approaching sounds of rumbling wheels and galloping hoofs.   The carriage of the Count, preceded by outriders and involved in a great cloud of luminous dust, comes dashing into town through the gateway.   The towns-people, whose seats border closely upon the public space, hastily start up and draw back.   The Stranger rises also, but holds his ground.]

The Host (*choking in the dust*).   Have a care!   Step back!

The Stranger (*standing with one foot upon his stool, which he has not moved*).   Ha, burgomaster!   I reject your advice, as *he* ignores your authority.   I will take care of myself.

[The carriage comes on, with every promise of grazing the Stranger's legs.   With his foot he tilts the stool against one of the forewheels. The stool is broken, the wheel is shattered, and the vehicle stops with a sudden wrench and jar.]

The COUNT (*rising in a rage from his seat*). What may you mean? Who are you to dare do this?

The STRANGER. One who comes from the breadth and freedom of the great outside world. One who asks the common rights of all—air, room. One who demands light to cast his shadow and space to let it fall.

The COUNT. Insolent varlet!—Seize him, my men!

The STRANGER (*drawing his sword*). Do not attempt it.

The COUNT'S NIECE (*rising from her place in the carriage*). Youth, you are bold.

The STRANGER (*saluting*). Girl, you are beautiful.

The COUNT'S NIECE. You should not say it.

The STRANGER. I think it. And what I think I speak.

The COUNT (*as he orders the disabled carriage to a halting advance toward his own gateway*). Sir, you shall hear more from this.

The STRANGER. And so shall you—all that your ears can take in.

[The carriage, with its occupants and attendants, disappears in the castle courtyard.]

The STRANGER (*to the dispersing Townspeople*). There, my friends! Laws are made for men, not men for laws. We are not born to fetters; we simply bow when they are placed upon us. We are not sent to fall in with arrangements that antedate our own arrival; the law for each of us is the imperious law of his own nature. Live your own life; grow; expand; develop along your own lines to the ut-

most limit of your own possibilities.   And lastly : as regards
all rules and regulations and their enforcement, to believe
in yourself and—to take your chances.   Ah, you are leaving?   Good evening.

[The men disperse toward the inn ; several of them enter
it.   There remain only the STRANGER and the HOST'S
DAUGHTER.   But the WATCHMAN'S WIFE again looks
down from her window, and presently the COUNT'S NIECE
appears on a balcony above the castle entrance.]

The HOST'S DAUGHTER. Sir, once more   your reckoning.

The STRANGER. Ah, my memory is so poor!   Yours
seems to be much better.   Come here. (*He lays his hand
upon her arm and draws her close to him.*)   What have we
in this pretty bag that is fastened so trimly about so trim a
waist?   Money, as I live!   Money ; a rarity!—let me but
touch it!   Ah, this is copper, and that is silver ; and this,
in the poor light we have, might pass for gold.

The HOST'S DAUGHTER. La! it is only a new penny.

The STRANGER. Then you may keep it.   As for these
others—these bits of silver . . .

The HOST'S DAUGHTER (*reaching for the coins, as he
jingles them in his closed hand*).   Sir, you are jesting.—
Again, your reckoning.

The STRANGER. Ah, what an admirable memory.   Can
you remember this?   (*He kisses her.*)   What else, indeed,
have I to pay you with?

The WATCHMAN'S WIFE (*at her window*).   Ah!   (*She
disappears.*)

The HOST'S DAUGHTER. Sir, return me my coins, and
pay me those ten groschen due.

The STRANGER. An admirable memory, yes; but it might be still more exact. Remember that you have received a kiss. Return it—return that first.

The HOST'S DAUGHTER. Why do you tease me?— Well, then; there! (*They kiss.*) But I know a youth in the castle courtyard who would not approve of this!

[The COUNT'S NIECE observes them from her balcony, but remains there. At the same moment, the HOST, who has left his strong box and a candle close to the open window of the inn, appears in the dusk under the linden-tree.]

The HOST. How, Minna! You kissing this cheating stranger in the dark? Go into the house at once.

The STRANGER. Ah, it is you! Meddling old fool, take this for your pains!

[He draws his sword and runs the old man through. The HOST, with a single groan, falls dead in the shadow of the linden-tree.]

The STRANGER. What has he left on the window-ledge? His strong box; and it is open. Quick!

[He extinguishes the candle and rifles the box. He hurriedly stuffs his pockets and returns to the open space, which the early moon is just beginning to light.]

The COUNT'S NIECE (*from her balcony*). Oh, sir, you have been hasty.

The STRANGER (*starting*). Ah, you honor me with your thoughts and your—glances! Hasty? Yes. There are times when every second counts.   (*With a shade of awakening prudence.*)   You blame my haste ;—in what ?

The COUNT'S NIECE. In attacking that poor old man.

The STRANGER (*relieved*). Is that all ?   In nothing else ?

The COUNT'S NIECE. Is he . . . is he . . . ?

The STRANGER. Never mind ; he does well where he is.   Shall you tell what you have seen ?

The COUNT'S NIECE. I ought to.

The STRANGER. Let it be a little secret between us.

The COUNT'S NIECE. But you told *my* secret.

The STRANGER. Yours ?   When ?   What was it ?

The COUNT'S NIECE. You pretend to have forgotten ? You said before all those people that I—that I was—was beautiful !

The STRANGER. Ha !   Is *that* your secret ?   It is an open one, believe me ;—as open as the sun.   And as dazzling.

The COUNT'S NIECE. Hush !   Some one approaches.

[She withdraws from her balcony.   The STRANGER retires into the shade.   Enter the WATCHMAN'S WIFE, who goes straight toward the tree.]

The WATCHMAN'S WIFE. Sir, you cannot hide.   I see you.

The STRANGER (*advancing*). Your eyes are as keen as they are beautiful.   With what are *you* come to tax me ?

The WATCHMAN'S WIFE. Oh, sir, you have done an evil thing.

The STRANGER (*wiping his sword and buttoning his pocket*). How do you mean ?   What have you seen ?

The WATCHMAN'S WIFE. I was at my window.   I—I saw you . . .

The STRANGER. You saw me what? Quick! quick!

The WATCHMAN'S WIFE. O, la! you are so masterful!
—I saw you kiss a young girl—fie! fie!

The STRANGER (*relieved*). Nothing more?

The WATCHMAN'S WIFE. Nothing more, I *hope*.

The STRANGER. You saw me kiss a young girl? A
young girl? How much younger than you are, I pray?
You (*drawing her closer*) are a young girl yourself. I must
kiss you too.

The WATCHMAN'S WIFE. Oh no! I am a married
woman. To kiss me would be most—Oh, shame! oh,
shame!

The STRANGER. A married woman, forsooth! Matched
to that doddering graybeard!—*there* is the shame.—
Once more,—once more!

The WATCHMAN'S WIFE. You are a wicked man—you
know you are. Leave me; some one is coming.

The STRANGER. What! will you fly me, and so soon?
Do you think I could not defend you?

[The WATCHMAN'S WIFE runs in the shadows toward
the town-gate; the STRANGER follows. Enter, from that
same direction, the WATCHMAN.]

The WATCHMAN. What, you evil youth!—pursuing a woman thus in a public place? Halt; halt, I command you!
(*He interposes his pike.*)

The STRANGER (*seizing the* WATCHMAN'S *own weapon
and turning it against him*). Die, dotard!

[The WATCHMAN sinks and expires in the shadow of the
gateway. The STRANGER casts away his pike and extinguishes his lantern. The COUNT'S NIECE, meanwhile, has
returned to her balcony.]

The Count's Niece. Oh, sir, another dark deed to be laid at your door.

The Stranger. My door? I have laid him at his own. Dark deed? All deeds are dark at night. But, one word: you shall not call me " sir."

The Count's Niece. No? What am I to call you? You have given me good cause to call you the worst of names.

The Stranger. In spite of that, call me the best. Call me—my love.

The Count's Niece. It is too soon.

The Stranger. Then call me Rudolph.

The Count's Niece. But—you kissed the wife before you killed the husband. And you kissed the maid before you kissed the wife.

The Stranger. Kissed? kissed? Of course I kissed. I have practised on other lips that I may do justice to yours. I cannot reach them yet, but I shall reach them soon, and I shall kiss them a hundred times between now and midnight—a kiss for every furlong of the road.

The Count's Niece. You are much too fast.

The Stranger. If we find ourselves going too fast, we will lengthen the time by going farther.

The Count's Niece. You have gone too far already.

The Stranger. Not so far but that you can follow me. — I have quenched one light, but—(looking into the court-yard)—but . . .

The Count's Niece. You have quenched two. Two lights and two lives.

The Stranger. But I see a third.

The Count's Niece. It is in our court-yard. They are putting a new wheel on the carriage, you bold fellow.

The STRANGER. Are the horses still in harness?

The COUNT'S NIECE. I fancy so. At least, they are not far away.

The STRANGER. Then send word to your men — (*He looks through the archway.*) They have more than a light; the smith has a fire. I will step within and tell them myself.

The COUNT'S NIECE. There is another door at the side; a small one — safer — unguarded.

The STRANGER. Am I the man to slink in at a side door?

The COUNT'S NIECE. And there are saddle-horses, too.

The STRANGER (*contemptuously*). Saddle-horses! — Yes, I have quenched two lights, as you say. Shall I quench a third?

The COUNT'S NIECE (*faltering*). A third? My — my uncle?

The STRANGER. You love him?

The COUNT'S NIECE. I hate him!

The STRANGER. Such a tender guardian?

The COUNT'S NIECE. Such an odious tyrant!

The STRANGER. Tyrant? Has he abused you?

The COUNT'S NIECE. Abused me? He has beaten me! And he has been dragging me round the country to marry me against my will.

The STRANGER. Oh, shameful! — You do not want to marry?

The COUNT'S NIECE. Not against my own will.

The STRANGER. Do you know your own will?

The COUNT'S NIECE. I believe so.

The STRANGER. Do you recognize your ideal when you meet it?

The COUNT'S NIECE. I do.

The STRANGER. Have you met it?

The COUNT'S NIECE. I have.

The STRANGER. Then go find your cloak — and your jewel case.

[He draws his sword and passes under the archway into the court-yard of the castle. Presently a tumult is heard within: there are cries, clashes of arms, flingings of burning brands. Then there issue through the doorway men-at-arms with pikes and linkmen with torches. The COUNT follows, and the STRANGER with his sword in one hand and a flaming brand in the other. All mingle in the scuffle of combat, and at the same time the tippling townsfolk issue from the tavern.]

The COUNT. Impudent swaggerer! now you shall learn your lesson!

The STRANGER. You, too, shall be taught all that lies in my power.

[They fight. The COUNT is forced back toward the fountain and falls wounded upon its steps.]

The STRANGER (*with his back against the church door*). Let no one dare to advance! Let no one think of taking me!

[A rash young halberdier mounts the church steps and is cut down for his pains, dying at the church door.]

The SCHOOLMASTER (*under the linden-tree*). Here lies the burgomaster dead — *he* has killed him!

The MASTER-BUILDER (*hastening across from the town-*

gate). There lies the watchman in his blood — *he* has slain him!

The GARDENER (*near the fountain*). That is like enough true; he has almost killed the count before our eyes!

The PRIEST. He has desecrated the church!

The MASTER-BUILDER (*as the* STRANGER *hurls his torch against the* COUNT'S *doorway*). And now he would fire the castle!

The STRANGER. I acknowledge all three — count, watchman, burgomaster. Try to understand what I have done, and thank me for it: I have freed you from all your tyrants great and small.

[At this moment the COUNT'S carriage is driven out through the doorway. Inside of it stands the COUNT'S NIECE, wrapped in a long mantle and armed with a heavy whip.]

The HOST'S DAUGHTER. He kisses me and runs away with her — he who has murdered my father!

The STRANGER (*his foot on the carriage step*). Think no more of your father. Think rather of a husband.

The WATCHMAN'S WIFE. He kisses me and runs away with her — he who has murdered my husband!

The STRANGER (*mounting into the carriage*). Think no more of your husband. Think of another one — and a younger one.

AN OLD WOMAN (*rushing forth from the crowd*). He has slain my son!

The HOST'S DAUGHTER (*screaming*). What! My Franz! (*Both women throw themselves on the dead body of the young halberdier.*)

The STRANGER (*seating himself beside the* COUNT'S NIECE). That is a detail.

The COUNT'S NIECE. My hero!

The STRANGER (*half-rising again*).   And now, my good people, farewell.   I have shown you the possibilities of life — the joys of untrammeled action.   It only remains for you to put my precepts into practice.   Entertain yourselves and one another.   Adieu.

The COUNT'S NIECE. But oh, Rudolph, that poor dead boy upon the church steps—surely there was no need of *that*.   See his mother, his betrothed; think of his twenty beautiful years all made naught in a moment . . .

The STRANGER. I act first and think afterward.   All heroes do.   I cannot be deterred by mere tears and groans; I cannot defer overmuch to human pity or to human relationships.   No hero does that.

The MASTER-BUILDER (*as he views the smoke and flame that roll out through the castle's entrance*).   And he has fired the castle too!—he would ruin so beautiful a monument of human industry and skill!   Oh, that a century of man's hand and brain should vanish in a single hour of hot-headed frenzy!

The STRANGER. I cannot respect the triumphs of human skill.   I cannot consider the continuity of art and of history.   I cannot show esteem for the mass of mere law-abiding plodders and their works.   No hero does that.

The COUNT'S NIECE. But surely you might have done with less of fury and of bloodshed.   You had but to use the private doorway.

The STRANGER. The private doorway!   And if I *had* used it, pray would you have come down to me?

The COUNT'S NIECE. N —— no. — But those other women . . .

13

The STRANGER. Those other women! If I had not kissed them, could I ever have kissed you?—as I do now.

The COUNT'S NIECE. N——no.

The STRANGER. Take my hand. Feel it; smell it; kiss it. Ah, what do you taste? What wets the laces at your wrist?

The COUNT'S NIECE. Blood.

The STRANGER. Ay, blood!—Now place your hand upon my heart: what do you feel?

The COUNT'S NIECE. Its throbs.

The STRANGER. Ay, its throbs. And every one of them sets more blood in motion than you could find in the sum of all the bodies round us—dead or living. Look about you. See these pale faces, these palsied arms. What are such creatures?—mere meat for me to feed upon. Yet I have spared them—I have even benefited them. I have shown them how to live; I have rescued them from the tyranny of social order, from the chains of—

The COUNT'S NIECE. Ah, noble, noble hero! With such as you I would go to the ends of the earth!

The STRANGER. Then let us depart. (*To the Towns-people.*) My friends, have you no cheer wherewith to speed Valor and Beauty on their way?

[A few voices combine in a faint and dubious crow.]

The COUNT (*dying upon the rim of the fountain*). Girl, I curse you!

The COUNT'S NIECE. Good. I have cursed you a hundred times.

The STRANGER (*clasping her to his breast*). Girl, you are after my own heart indeed! What is your name?

The COUNT'S NIECE. That is a detail.—Where are we going?

The STRANGER. That is another.   (*He catches the whip from her hands and begins to belabor the coachman's back.*) Forward! forward!

[The carriage pushes through the awed and bewildered crowd, rattles across the square and under the town-gate, and rolls out into the open country and the night.]

IN SUCH A NIGHT—

IN SUCH A NIGHT—

PERSONS.

The PROREGE of ARCOPIA.   The CHATELAINE of LA TRI-
Miss AURELIA WEST.   NITÉ.
The CHEVALIER of PENSIE- Mr. GEORGE OCCIDENT.
RI-VANI.

The balustrade of a classic terrace set with potted aloes
and banked with rhododendrons. Steps lead up to a Corin-
thian portico adorned with Pompeian frescoes, and down
to a vast basin enlivened by many pleasure-craft. On one
hand a long quadruple colonnade, pierced in its middle
by a great triumphal arch, backs up an enormous golden
figure that towers mightily above the water; on the other
a fretted dome rises through the early evening air with an
aspect of tranquil expectation. On the opposite side of the
basin, similar terraces and porticos at once round out and
enclose the shadowed whiteness of the scene.

Present: the CHATELAINE, AURELIA WEST and the
PROREGE—a man of fifty, who wears a pointed beard
and carries himself with an air of serene and amicable
condescension.

AURELIA. The consecrated moment is at hand. A great
light is about to shine and your conversion about to be

accomplished. There is no one but has yielded to the force and beauty of the evangel so soon to address you.

The CHATELAINE. I am in your hands — as ever. Work your will upon me.

AURELIA. Then I begin. The universe is mine to command, and it is my design to make it freely yours. (*She waves her hand aloft.*) There! do you see that?

The CHATELAINE (*looking into the deepening blue of the sky*). The evening star? I see it — yes. But I have often seen it from my own doorstep.

AURELIA. — Away up in your snowy and secluded little valley, you would say, among your broken pines and your riven mountain-peaks. But you shall soon see other stars that you have never seen before — either there or elsewhere. And for every one that twinkles overhead to-night, a hundred more shall twinkle beneath our feet. Look!

[The walls of the basin, throughout their whole vast sweep, are suddenly outlined by thousands of tiny lights which, with a tremulous eagerness, hasten to double themselves in the flood beneath. A moment afterward a second line of living light runs swiftly along cornices, attics and pediments, and rescues from the descending darkness long rows of shining statues set high in air. Other stars appear in the heavens.]

The PROREGE (*leaning in absorption upon the balustrade*). Strophe and antistrophe: the choir celestial and the choir terrestrial.

The CHATELAINE. Thanks for your stars. And the wake of that gondola multiplies every one of them into a yellow thousand. Thanks for them all. But —

AURELIA. But stars are not enough, you would say. Then you shall have more than stars.

[She waves her hand toward the colonnade. Through its ranks of thick-set pillars a vast pale disk is seen to be rising slowly above a limitless expanse of water.]

The CHATELAINE. O, conjurer!—But, after all, it is only our old friend, the moon. We have seen her rise over many and many a lake—you and I together.

AURELIA. Ingrate! One moon, then, is not enough. Well, you shall have a hundred: moons that do not rise, but simply — come. See!

[Upon the instant many scores of white globes blossom dazzlingly in midair; they flood with their moony light the long stretches of white arcades and porticos and mingle their opalescent gleam with the yellow ripples that dapple the bosom of the great basin.]

The PROREGE (*with a fond paternal glance toward* AURELIA). The harmony of the spheres: who could evoke it or apprehend it save one in full accord with her environment?

The CHATELAINE (*with a mounting interest*). Your moons are enchanting. Enchanting,—but —

AURELIA. But! but!—My hundred moons are not enough? Are you meaning to ask me for something more?

The CHATELAINE. Yes. Give me (for you can give me anything at all)—give me—the sun.

AURELIA. You shall have it. Quick!—shut your eyes!

[From some point high above the spectacle (the spectacle so far as yet revealed) a great red eye glares suddenly through the darkness and sends down from across the basin a wide and blinding shaft of light.]

The CHATELAINE (*starting, and covering her eyes*). Ah, magician!

[When the CHATELAINE looks again, four or five other lights have joined the first. They overlace the heavens; they sweep with immense rapidity the sculptured sky-lines of many long-drawn palaces; they accomplish the sudden evocation (from the darkness) of unseen domes and unsuspected towers.]

The CHATELAINE. It is magnificent, but—it is not the sun. You have given me comets, and comets will not suffice. (*With kindling enthusiasm.*) Give me the sun—the sun! Try again. Surely, one failure in such a task should bring you neither discredit nor discouragement.

AURELIA. Very well. I will make a second attempt.—Look!

[From above the serried figures that crest the colonnade a thin red line of light rushes heavenward and bursts into a broad glory of yellow and purple and green.]

The CHATELAINE. Ah! that is the s—— (*A second rocket rises and bursts. And a third.*) No, no; that is not the sun—there can be but one sun. You are giving me meteors merely. But you can achieve the sun for us yet: you are on your own ground—you are the wielder of your

own will. In the accomplishment of such a wonder even
a second failure need not disgrace you. Come, then;
come. Your meteors are glorious, but give us the greater
glory.

The PROREGE (*rapt*). Give us the Greatest Glory.

AURELIA (*with a deep breath of invincible determination*).
I will. (*She throws out both hands toward the other end
of the basin.*) Behold it!

[An invisible band of musicians has begun to play; their
sonorous and voluminous tones are wafted rhythmically
through the length and breadth of the court. At the same
moment two great fountains throw up their lofty and clus-
tered sprays in changing columns of red and amber and
green. Between these two fountains a third, vaster than
either and peopled with many fantastic figures, is suddenly
redeemed from the dusk by a quick-flung pencil of lilac
light. Its waters fall plashing over many steps, and far
above the pride of its topmost figure a vast dome, loftier
than all else and more dazzling than all else combined,
suddenly flashes through the blueness of the night. It is
ribbed with light, and crowned with fire, and girdled with
torches; it appropriates and concentrates all the splendor
and melody and magnificence of the entire spectacle.]

AURELIA. *There* is the Greatest Glory.   [Silence.

The PROREGE (*after an interval*). Alas, poor Arcopia!

The CHATELAINE (*softly*). Its lustre is dimmed.

AURELIA (*raingloriously*). What can be cited, between
all the borders of Adria and of Illyria? Arcopia Felix is
eclipsed!

The PROREGE (*leaning meditatively upon the balustrade*).
That is true.   [Silence.

AURELIA (*to the* CHATELAINE). The stage is set and lighted.   Do you wish me to summon the performers ?

The CHATELAINE. Many, many thousands must be here already.   All round me I hear the click and shuffle of myriads of feet, the night air is full of voices, and every lightest breeze from the water brings the sound of music to our ears.   Surely the whole world has assembled.   Look! Behind those aloes a group of men in yellow turbans; under that portico others arrayed in fez and scimitar.

AURELIA. *They* cannot fill such a stage—in such a night; nor could thousands more like them—or unlike them. And since we ourselves have been debarred from taking a spectacular part —— Oh, why did his Highness refuse ? The Rajah of Kajama made a triumphal progress through these noble canals; the Exarch of Albania was received in state beneath that blazing dome.   The Prorege of Arcopia, and he alone, has failed of the honors that—

The CHATELAINE. Hush! our great friend's incognito must remain inviolate.   You would not betray him by a rash and vain ambition.   Recall his unfortunate experience at Rome . . .

AURELIA. I say no more.   We remain nonentities, then, —with all the others.   The stage stands vacant, the spectacle incomplete.   And one element more—the essential element—is missing : the one that makes the world go round!   Without that element, all is a mere row of valueless ciphers.   But put *that* figure at the head—!   If only *he* were here!

The CHATELAINE. He, Aurelia ? (*She seizes* AURELIA's *hand.*)   My dear girl!—and you never told me!

AURELIA. You misunderstand me, Bertha.   It is *I* who would wish to seize *your* hand.

The CHATELAINE (*turning away with a sudden blush*).

Do not make another such attempt, Aurelia. Let us do nothing to recall those old days at La Trinité. I have forgotten Count Fin-de-Siècle; I have forgotten Baron Zeitgeist. I was but a poor child of nature in those simple times.

AURELIA. Nor are you completely a child of artifice yet, my dear.—And you have forgotten the Marquis of Tempo-Rubato as well?

The CHATELAINE. I have kept his picture, but I seldom think of him.

AURELIA (*after a long and thoughtful pause*). If only *he* were here!

The CHATELAINE. I beg, Aurelia, that you will not refer to the marquis again. When we parted at La Trinité we parted forever.

AURELIA. I am not speaking of the marquis. I am speaking of *him*.

The CHATELAINE. Of *him?*

AURELIA. Of him. I do not speak his name, because I have never heard it. But between us he needs no name, I think.

The CHATELAINE (*blushing again*). Be careful, Aurelia. Do not ask the impossible once more.

AURELIA. The impossible?   Nothing is impossible — here! (*After a pause.*) Where did we first see him? At Caprile. He gave up his room to us at the inn. And before we awoke in the morning he was half way over the mountains to Cortina. Where did we meet him next? At Amalfi. He was painting the cathedral. Are there not as worthy things to paint all round us here?—Where did we encounter him the third time? Where? where?

The CHATELAINE (*stammering*). I—I have forgotten.

AURELIA. You remember perfectly. Where? where?

The CHATELAINE. In the Roman Forum.

AURELIA. In the Roman Forum — right. What was he doing?

The CHATELAINE. Sketching the ruins of the Palatine.

AURELIA. Sketching the ruins of the Palatine — wrong. He was resurrecting the Palatine — the Palatine of Caligula. It was a work of taste, of knowledge, of imagination. How he heaped up that magnificence and glorified it! — But there are grander things all round us here.

The CHATELAINE. Perhaps you are right.

AURELIA. I know I am right. And here he ought to be. — Come; you think of him now and then?

The CHATELAINE (*in a tremor*). Now and then.

AURELIA. And you have dreamed of him more than once?

The CHATELAINE. Not more than once.

AURELIA. Ah! Once?

The CHATELAINE. Once.

AURELIA. What was your — ? But, no; that dream shall remain your own.

The PROREGE (*coming out of his reverie*). Time is passing. The throng is moving on. Much more must await our attentive senses. Let us move about too, for a little. We have several moments to spare before the one that must find us again upon this spot.

AURELIA. The moment that must find us again upon this spot, your Highness?

The PROREGE. Come.

[They pass away. A moment later a gondola full of colored lanterns and tinkling mandolins glides up to the landing-stage. Mr. GEORGE OCCIDENT alights and ascends to the terrace. He is followed by the CHEVALIER of PENSIERI-VANI.]

OCCIDENT. Have I redeemed my promise?

The CHEVALIER. You have more than redeemed it, my dear Occident.

OCCIDENT. I have levied upon the whole world. I have brought you a gondola from Venice, and terraces and quays and bridges from Dresden and Florence, and balustrades and aloes from the Pamfili Gardens—

The CHEVALIER. I recognize them.

OCCIDENT. —and colonnades from Rome, and porticos from Athens, and domes and towers from Toledo and Seville, and fountains from Versailles—

The CHEVALIER. But Versailles could show no such splendor of color.

OCCIDENT. —and far-flashing lights that not all the coasts you have skirted can parallel, and banners that might easily out-fête Paris itself, and a dome whose bright and sudden coming outshines St. Peter's own; and people, people, people—in such variety as even no Galata Bridge could hope to rival. See; those Arabs striding along in white burnooses; presently we shall have some green-skirted Egyptians, or some American aborigines in ochre and eagle-feathers—my ancestral stock. And to-morrow you shall see other peoples from far beyond your ken. They will wear tallow in their curls, or they will bind bark fringes round their waists and knees and ankles, or they will shriek and caper in next to nothing at all. And to-morrow noon you shall hear my wife sing the Inflammatus yonder in that white hall beneath those bursting bombs.

The CHEVALIER. Those bombs, those sunbursts — where do they fall? What lies beyond that colonnade?

OCCIDENT. A lake.

The CHEVALIER. And what bounds its further side? Ah, you do not know — we are both too newly come. But let us be generous; let us rear there a snowy chain of mountain-peaks — the spectacle lacks nothing else.

OCCIDENT (*to himself*). His thoughts are on the mountain-peaks! (*Aloud.*) Ah!

The CHEVALIER. And the city which has reared this majestic manifestation — a city that I have not yet seen: how can we figure it save as a place of beauty —compacted of such glorious streets and palaces as must be fit for a right noble people?

OCCIDENT. A —— ah!

The CHEVALIER. And that people, I think, we have no choice but to endow with decorum and serenity and dignity and high resolve and noble purpose and ——

OCCIDENT. A —— a —— ah!

The CHEVALIER. Your wife, you say, sings here to-morrow? For you, then, this magnificent thing is complete. For me . . .

OCCIDENT. Make it complete. Make your life complete. Make yourself complete.

The CHEVALIER. The Prorege was not to be alone, I think. We are in advance of the time, I see.

OCCIDENT. Alone? I do not know. I wish that she might be here too.

The CHEVALIER. And I.

OCCIDENT. You saw her last at ——?

The CHEVALIER. At Geneva. And lost her promptly in the summer's hurly-burly. Her presence here to-night would round out everything to perfection.

OCCIDENT. She would add the one touch of nature — would add it to your thousand touches of art.

The CHEVALIER. It is the one touch needed.

OCCIDENT. She could give it.

The CHEVALIER. I should not evade it.

OCCIDENT. You have visited La Trinité?

The CHEVALIER. I went there once with the Queen — that summer fortnight among the High Alps. The Chatelaine was absent; she had gone to Paris.

OCCIDENT. To Paris? For the touch of nature?

The CHEVALIER. Paris did not spoil her. Nothing has spoiled her. Nothing could spoil her. I only ask to find her here.

OCCIDENT. In such a night ——

The CHEVALIER. In such a night.

[AURELIA, the CHATELAINE and the PROREGE return.]

The PROREGE. Welcome, my dear Occident; welcome, my dear Cavaliere! Our little party is now complete. This is not the first party that I have made complete — as my dear Occident may recall.

OCCIDENT. I do, with gratitude, Altezza. It is you who have made me what I am, in more senses than one.

The PROREGE. Yes, my dear fellow; it was I who gave you an education and a wife.

[The PROREGE presents the CHEVALIER and OCCIDENT to the CHATELAINE and AURELIA WEST. The CHATELAINE and the CHEVALIER bow in silence.]

AURELIA (*talking very loud and very fast*). Ah, *vous voici joliment bien ensemble!* — master and pupil I mean, of course. Master and pupil — what else could I mean? Yes, I have heard about it. Nothing of the sort was ever done for me; I was left to work out my own salvation — to say nothing of that of another . . .

The PROREGE. Make it, rather, pupil and master. It is

14

I who am now on the learner's bench.   It is to my former disciple that I am indebted for this view of the wider world —

OCCIDENT. The slightest possible return!

The PROREGE. — a view that has dimmed the Arcopian glories forever. And you (*to* AURELIA), you, too, have lent a hand.

AURELIA (*with a nervous eagerness*).   But there are glories that never can be dimmed: the glories of the High Alps — the glories of La Trinité and of its mistress.   And so, my dear Bertha — (*She looks round, suddenly.*)   Why, where *is* Bertha?   Ah, there she stands yonder in the shadow of that big aloe.   I am with you at once, my love . . . (*She moves toward the* CHATELAINE *and the* CHEVALIER.)

The PROREGE (*intercepting her*). Mademoiselle, the fountains are playing, the music is swelling, these myriads of lights are glittering, the peoples of the world are footing it past us; the spectacle will not last forever — let us enjoy the brief moment that it does.   Take my arm; I will show you the moonlight as it wavers round the prow of that gondola; I will give you a better opportunity to hear those mandolins — which are receiving the tribute of attention from all ears save those that they are addressing.   Follow us, Occident, and let your men arrange your poor old friend's cushions properly — he has been so long upon his feet.

AURELIA. But tell me; how do you call that gentleman?

The PROREGE. You heard his name.

AURELIA. But where does he come from?

The PROREGE. From a far country — like myself.

AURELIA. But who is he — what is he?

The PROREGE. A friend of mine, — a very dear friend of mine.   That should be enough.

AURELIA. I heard the name, yes; but I never heard it before.

The PROREGE. Your friend has heard it.

AURELIA. Bertha? Impossible!

The PROREGE. You contradict me?

AURELIA. Pardon, Altezza. But she has never mentioned it to me.

The PROREGE. She has kept it for herself. But you have had other names to make free with, have you not?

AURELIA. Your Highness rebukes me!— me, whom she has found so good and true a friend!

The PROREGE. I rebuke you? Not at all. No, no; there must not be the least touch of severity — in such a night. But there is this to bear in mind: *your* opportunity you have already had —

AURELIA. I know; at La Trinité itself.

The PROREGE. — and to-night's opportunity is mine. I have allowed you to set the stage; you must allow me to direct the little drama. Do you not see why our dear girl asked so much?— and why even the sun, moon and stars were not enough? Did you not apprehend that the greatest glory was soon to be eclipsed by the Greatest Glory of All?

AURELIA (*looking backward*). I am a poor blind creature, indeed!

OCCIDENT (*who is overtaking them, and into whose face she speaks*). One might well be blinded in such a blaze of splendor;— the fountains an untamable tumult of color, and six great sunbursts— see them!— rising all at once!

[The three move toward the gondola. Presently the CHEVALIER and the CHATELAINE follow.]

AURELIA (*holding out her hands to them, impulsively*). In such a night! —

The CHEVALIER. In such a night? No such night has ever been before, believe me.

[The Five enter the gondola and glide toward the great golden dome. In the general brilliancy their faces, their voices, their lights and their music are merged and lost.]

THE END.

www.ingramcontent.com/pod-product-compliance
Lightning Source LLC
Chambersburg PA
CBHW030820270326
41928CB00007B/819